Gods, Goddesses, and Mythology

Volume 10

Sigurd–Zeus

Marshall Cavendish
New York • London • Singapore

Marshall Cavendish
99 White Plains Road
Tarrytown, New York 10591

www.marshallcavendish.us

© 2005 Marshall Cavendish Corporation

All rights reserved. No part of this book may be reproduced or
utilized in any form or by any means electronic or mechanical,
including photocopying, recording, or by any information storage
and retrieval system, without prior written permission from the
publisher and copyright holder.

Library of Congress Cataloging-in-Publication Data

Gods, goddesses, and mythology/editor, C. Scott Littleton.
    p. cm.
    Includes bibliographical references and index.
    ISBN 0-7614-7559-1 (set : alk. paper)
1. Mythology--Encyclopedias. I. Littleton, C. Scott. II. Marshall
Cavendish Corporation. III. Title.

    BL312.G64 2005
    201'.3'03--dc22

    2004040758

Printed and bound in China

09 08 07 06 05   6 5 4 3 2

ISBN 0-7614-7559-1 (set)
ISBN 0-7614-7569-9 (vol. 10)

General Editor
C. Scott Littleton, Occidental College, Los Angeles

Marshall Cavendish
Project Editor: Marian Armstrong
Editorial Director: Paul Bernabeo
Production Manager: Alan Tsai

Brown Reference Group
Project Editor: Chris King
Editors: Andrew Campbell, Henry Russell, Lee Stacy, Dawn
    Titmus, Tom Webber
Designer: Steve Wilson
Picture Researcher: Helen Simm
Cartographer: Mark Walker
Indexer: Kay Ollerenshaw
Managing Editor: Tim Cooke

Picture Credits

Cover: Greek vase depicting Athena. **AKG**, Erich Lessing

AKG: 1303, 1342, 1345, 1386, 1393, 1413, 1417, Erich Lessing
1307, 1312, 1343, 1349, 1371, 1423, Nimatallah 1418, Jean-Louis
Nou 1392; **Art Archive:** Bodleian Library, Oxford 1339, Dagli
Orti 1344, 1389, 1415, Galleria Nazionale, Parma/Dagli Orti
1357, Historiska Museet, Stockholm/Dagli Orti 1404, 1405,
Museo di Castelvecchio/Dagli Orti 1436, National Archaeological
Museum, Athens/Dagli Orti 1376, National Gallery, London/
John Webb 1338, Neuschwanstein Castle, Germany/Dagli Orti
1301, Salamanca University/Dagli Orti 1334, Nicolas Sapieha
1428, Victoria & Albert Museum/Eileen Tweedy 1346;
Brown Reference Group: 1324, 1330, 1408, 1431;
Bridgeman Art Library: Chris Beetles, London 1401, Archives
Charmet 1321, Dominican Convent, Dubrovnik 1317,
Hermitage, St Petersburg 1373, Musee des Beaux-Arts, Calais
1306, Museum of Fine Arts, Budapest 1351, Muzeum Norodowe,
Warsaw 1434, Nationalmuseet, Copenhagen 1367, Private
Collection 1319, 1337, 1363, Royal Library, Copenhagen 1632,
Samuel & Mary R Bancroft Memorial 1398, Victoria & Albert
Museum, London 1355, York Museums Trust 1372; **Corbis:**
Archivo Iconografico SA 1332, 1385, Yann Arthus-Bertrand 1399,
Christie's Images 1414, Araldo de Luca 1314, 1425, Michael
Freeman 1347, Lindsay Hebberd 1326, Historical Picture Archive
1381, 1390, Dave G Houser 1308, Andrea Jemolo 1377, Christine
Kolisch 1323, Charles & Josette Lenars 1329, Francis G Mayer
1433, Carmen Redondo 1331, Kevin Schafer 1432, Hubert
Stadler 1365, State Russian Museum 1320, Adam Woolfitt 1391;
EMPICS: 1437; **Lebrecht Collection:** 1400, Interfoto, Munich
1305, 1409; **Mary Evans Picture Library:** 1302, 1311, 1350,
1361, 1366, 1368, 1397, 1406, 1407, 1430, Arthur Rackham
Collection 1359; **NASA:** 1396, 1410; **NOAA:** 1403;
Photodisc: 1322; **Photos.com:** 1304, 1309, 1313, 1316, 1327,
1328, 1333, 1340, 1341, 1380, 1394, 1429; **Photos12.com:** ARJ
1356, 1374; **Scala Archives:** Gregorian Museum of Etruscan
Art, Vatican 1379, Musee Jacquemart-Andre, Paris 1354, Musees
Royaux des Beaux-Arts, Brussels 1375, Museo Archaeologico,
Palermo 1435, Palazzo Vecchio, Florence 1395; **Science Photo
Library:** Pekka Parviainen 1335; **Rene Seindal:** 1411; **South
American Pictures:** Chris Sharp 1383, 1384; **Jim Steinhart:**
1438; **Topham:** 1370, 1420, 1422, British Museum/HIP 1352,
1369, 1426, Charles Walker 1427; **Werner Forman Archive:**
1315, 1336, David Bernstein, New York 1310, Museum of the
American Indian, Heye Foundation 1348, National Museum,
Copenhagen 1360, Statens Historiska Museum, Stockholm 1364,
1402, 1424; **World Art Kiosk:** University of California/
Kathleen Cohen 1353, 1387, 1419, University of California/John
R Ross 1421

CONTENTS

SIGURD

Sigurd was the hero of one of the most famous and influential legends in Germanic mythology. His story involves a dragon, cursed treasure, marriage, betrayal, and death, and includes the central themes of Norse mythology: courage, loyalty, and acceptance of one's fate.

Sigurd came from a warrior dynasty based in a legendary Hunland, which may have been the homeland of the Huns, a real-life warrior people who dominated central Europe between about 370 and 455 CE. Sigurd's grandfather was Völsung, said to be the great-grandson of Odin, the chief Norse god. Sigurd's father was Sigmund, the only man able to draw from an oak tree a sword that had been pushed into it by Odin himself. The sword helped Sigmund win many wars, but during one battle Odin appeared and smashed the sword with his spear. Sigmund's time had come: without his sword, his enemies overcame him and left him mortally wounded. Before he died, however, Sigmund gave his broken sword to his wife, Hjördís, and predicted that the child with which she was pregnant, Sigurd, would grow up to become a great hero.

Hjördís was taken into protection by Álf, a prince of Denmark, whom she married after giving birth to her son. Sigurd grew up in the Danish royal court, and as a youth became renowned for his strength, courage, and intelligence. His tutor was the smith Regin, who taught Sigurd the skills of rune-writing, languages, weaponry, and fighting. Regin also encouraged Sigurd to choose one of the king's horses for himself. When Sigurd went to inspect the royal horses, he encountered an old, one-eyed man wearing a cloak and a broad-brimmed hat. The old man was none other than Odin, who helped Sigurd choose a beautiful gray horse, Grani, the offspring of Odin's eight-legged horse, Sleipnir.

Slaying the dragon

Regin was determined to use Sigurd for his own ends. He told the youth the story of his own brothers, Fafnir and Otr, and how Fafnir had come to possess a huge hoard of treasure, which—since Fafnir was a shape-shifter—he guarded in the form of a dragon (see box, page 1303). Regin goaded Sigurd into stealing the dragon's treasure by questioning the youth's courage. Sigurd agreed to help the smith, but first told him that he required a sword fit for the task. Regin forged one and then another sword using all his skill, but Sigurd smashed both weapons against the smith's anvil. Finally, the youth obtained the broken pieces of his father's sword from his mother, with which Regin forged a blade so strong that it sliced the anvil in half.

Regin accompanied Sigurd on his journey to Fafnir's lair. Once there, the smith pointed out a track made by the dragon when it came down to drink from a lake. He advised Sigurd to dig a hole for himself in this track, and to wait until the dragon passed over him before piercing its heart with the sword. Regin then left Sigurd to make his hole, but presently Odin appeared again. He warned Sigurd that, if he made just one hole, he would drown in the dragon's blood. Far better, the god advised, to make several other holes into which the blood could flow. Sigurd heeded Odin's words and, when he killed the dragon, he survived despite being covered in the monster's blood. Regin then emerged from his hiding place. He asked Sigurd to cut out the dragon's heart and roast it for him to eat. Sigurd did as instructed but, sucking his thumb after burning it, tasted Fafnir's blood and magically began to understand the twittering of birds on a nearby tree. The birds told Sigurd that the dragon's blood had made him invulnerable, save for a spot between his shoulders that had been covered with a leaf. They warned him to kill Regin, who, they said, intended to betray Sigurd. The birds also said that Sigurd should eat the dragon's heart himself, take the treasure, and journey to Hindafjall, where a beautiful maiden lay asleep.

Sigurd did as the birds told him, killing Regin. Arriving at Hindafjall, he saw a castle surrounded by a blazing fire.

Right: This detail from a 19th-century German painting depicts the scene from Wagner's opera Siegfried *in which the hero kills the dragon Fafnir.*

The fearless hero urged his horse Grani through the flames, and once in the castle came across the sleeping maiden. This was Brynhild, a Valkyrie, one of the maidens who served Odin by choosing mortal warriors to join him in his heavenly hall, Valhalla. Brynhild had offended Odin by letting a young warrior live. Her punishment was to marry a mortal and become mortal herself. Sigurd woke the maiden either by piercing the armor she was wearing or by removing a thorn stuck in the back of her hand. He duly fell in love with Brynhild; she said that Sigurd was the mortal Odin intended her to marry.

The next part of the myth is confusing, in part because there is a gap in the narrative of the surviving sources. For some reason, Sigurd left his love and journeyed to the palace of a king named Gjúki. He got on so well with the king and his family that Gjúki's wife, the sorceress Grímhild, gave him a potion of forgetfulness that erased his memory of Brynhild and made him fall in love instead

with the king's daughter, Gudrún. The couple soon married and, at their wedding feast, Gjúki's eldest sons Gunnar and Hogni swore blood-brotherhood with Sigurd. Queen Grímhild then arranged for Sigurd to help Gunnar gain a wife, too—the woman Grímhild decided on being none other than Brynhild. However, only Sigurd's horse Grani, carrying Sigurd himself, was capable of jumping through the wall of fire surrounding Brynhild's castle. Grímhild had a magical solution: she taught the two men the art of shape-shifting, so that Sigurd took on Gunnar's form. "Gunnar" then leaped through the flames and asked Brynhild to become his wife. Brynhild accepted, even though she loved Sigurd. Odin's prophecy, however, had been that the man she would marry would be able to jump through the fire. As far as the former Valkyrie knew, this man was Gunnar. Sigurd's memory of his love for Brynhild returned only at the wedding feast to celebrate her marriage to Gunnar. Ever a man of honor, he said nothing.

Truth and death

The fatal turning point in the tale was an argument that took place one day between Brynhild and Gudrún. Brynhild claimed that her husband was braver than Gudrún's: had he not, after all, ridden through a ring of fire to claim her? Gudrún answered that it was Sigurd, not Gunnar, who had jumped through the flames. Brynhild became enraged at this news and, in revenge, urged Gunnar to kill Sigurd. Gunnar found himself in a difficult situation: he could not personally kill his blood brother, but at the same time he wanted to satisfy his wife and gain Sigurd's treasure. His solution was to persuade his younger brother, Gutthorm, to murder Sigurd for him. There are two versions of how Gutthorm carried out the deed. In one account, he benefited from Gudrún's trust in him. She approached her younger brother and, concerned that her husband might be at risk from attack, told him to guard the one spot on his body that was not invulnerable. She even sewed a leaf of red silk between the shoulders of Sigurd's jacket so that Gutthorm might know which place he was to protect. Sigurd then went on a hunting expedition with Gutthorm and his other brothers-in-law. Alone with Sigurd in a forest, Gutthorm plunged his sword right through the hero's vulnerable spot. Sigurd died valiantly, recognizing that Gutthorm was only doing the bidding of Gunnar and Brynhild. In another account, Gutthorm crept into Sigurd's

Left: In this 19th-century book illustration, Sigurd helps to forge the magic sword with which he will slay the dragon Fafnir. In the background is Regin the smith.

The Curse of the Ring

In order to persuade Sigurd to help him steal the dragon Fafnir's treasure, Regin told his charge the story of how his brother had acquired it. The brother of Regin and Fafnir, called Otr, was a shape-shifter who liked to take on the form of an otter. He was killed by the god Loki, who failed to realize that the creature was really a man. As wergild (an ancient form of compensation for murder), Hreidmar, father of Regin and Fafnir, demanded enough treasure to cover his dead son's body. Loki obliged by stealing gold from a dwarf named Andvari. Ignoring the dwarf's pleas, Loki even took the ring from his finger. In response, Andvari cursed both his stolen ring and the treasure, proclaiming that death and destruction would fall on anyone who owned it. This curse was indeed borne out in the Sigurd story: whoever possessed the ring—by turns, it passed from Hreidmar to Fafnir, Sigurd, Brynhild, and Gudrún—or the treasure—owned at various times by Hreidmar, Fafnir, Sigurd, Gunnar, and Hogni—suffered tragedy. The story of a cursed ring was a major influence on numerous European works of art, music, and literature.

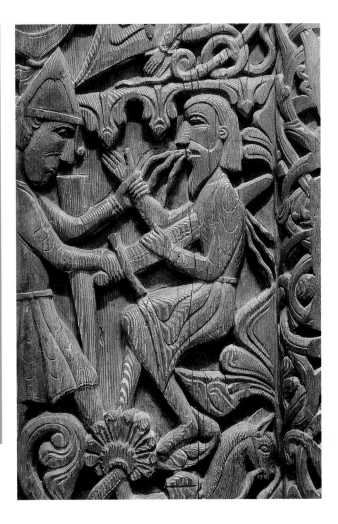

Right: Dated about 1200 CE, this carving from a church in Norway depicts Sigurd slaying the smith Regin.

bedroom and killed the hero as he slept. Sigurd woke up as the sword went through him, however. He reached for his own sword and threw it at Gutthorm, slicing him in two.

Sigurd's death led to further bloodshed. Brynhild threw herself on Sigurd's funeral pyre out of love for him. One account tells how she followed Sigurd into Hel, the land of the dead. Gudrún bitterly mourned the death of her husband, but in time was persuaded by her family to marry Brynhild's brother Atli. Atli coveted Sigurd's treasure, which had passed into the hands of Gunnar and his brother Hogni, but the brothers learned of his intention to kill them. A war broke out in which Gudrún fought on the side of her brothers. Atli killed the brothers; in turn, Gudrún killed him and the sons she had borne him. Sigurd's treasure, meantime, had been buried by Gunnar and Hogni at the bottom of the Rhine River. According to the myth, it remains there to this day.

Sources

The Sigurd story is found in the 12th-century Icelandic collection known as the *Poetic Edda*, but its fullest account is in the *Völsunga Saga*, also composed in Iceland in the

13th century. This saga contains the most extensive description of Sigurd, "who far surpassed other men in courtesy, in all fit behavior," and whose "body was beautifully proportioned in height and breadth, and in every respect, most handsome." A number of other poems add detail to the tale. The poem "Fáfnismál," for instance, records a conversation between Sigurd and the dying dragon Fafnir, while the poem "Reginsmál" tells how Sigurd sought vengeance for his father, Sigmund, by killing those who had murdered him. Archaeological evidence from the Viking period (9th–11th centuries CE) also contains motifs from the story. For example, a carved stone in Andreas, on the Isle of Man off the northwest coast of England, depicts Sigurd roasting Fafnir's heart and putting his burned thumb in his mouth while Grani looks on.

Sigurd appears in early British literature. His tale is sung by a minstrel in the Old English epic poem *Beowulf*, believed to have been written between 700 and 750 CE. Sigurd also has a central role in two works of German literature, in which his name is Siegfried. One is the early 16th-century poem *Das Lied vom hürnen Seyfrid* ("The Song of Noble Siegfried"), which relates how the hero

Above: The Rhine River in Germany. According to legend, Sigurd's treasure lies on the riverbed to this day.

released a maiden from the clutches of a dragon. The other is the *Nibelungenlied* ("Song of the Nibelungs"), written around 1200 by an unknown Austrian poet and named for a mountain people, the Nibelungs, whom Siegfried conquers. In the poem, Siegfried marries the beautiful Kriemhild by winning the favor of her brother Gunther. He does this by impersonating Gunther to seduce the princess Brunhild on his behalf. Brunhild later discovers the deception and arranges for Gunther's kinsman, Hagen, to murder the hero. Kriemhild exacts a terrible revenge on her family, which results in the deaths of all her brothers and many others besides—including Kriemhild herself. Kriemhild's revenge is unlike the Norse story of Sigurd, and was based on historical fact—the attacks on the Burgundian kingdom along the Rhine by the Hun leader Attila (known as Atli in the *Völsunga Saga*), who ruled between 434 and 453 CE.

Themes, parallels, and influences
Sigurd is the archetypal Norse hero who demonstrates courage, endurance, and loyalty to his kin. Scholars have a good idea that these were qualities prized by Germanic peoples of northern Europe, since Roman historian Tacitus (c. 56–120 CE) mentioned them in his description of those peoples, the *Germania*. Sigurd's other vital quality as a Norse hero is his acceptance of his fate. Time and again in the *Völsunga Saga* Sigurd calmly expresses his knowledge

of his own impending death. Such worldly pessimism was a feature of Norse mythology, finding its greatest expression in beliefs about Ragnarok, the apocalypse that awaited both gods and mortals.

The Sigurd story contains elements common to other myths. Sigurd's invulnerability, marred by his one weak spot, connects him to the Greek hero Achilles, who was also invulnerable save for his heel. In addition, the tale of Sigurd's father, Sigmund, pulling Odin's sword from the tree draws a parallel with the British legend of King Arthur, who drew the magic sword Excalibur from a stone. The Sigurd story has also influenced numerous other tales, from the fairy story of Sleeping Beauty to *The Lord of the Rings* by J. R. R. Tolkien (1892–1973), and The Ring Cycle, a series of four operas by German classical composer Richard Wagner (1813–1883).

ANDREW CAMPBELL

Bibliography
Cavendish, Richard, ed. *Man, Myth, and Magic*. New York: Marshall Cavendish, 1995.
Davidson, H. R. Ellis *Scandinavian Mythology*. London: Hamlyn, 1982.
Orchard, Andy. *Cassell's Dictionary of Norse Myth and Legend*. London: Cassell, 1997.
Rosenburg, Donna. *World Mythology*. Chicago: NTC/ Contemporary Publishing Group, Inc., 1999.
Warner, Marina, ed. *World of Myths*. London: The British Museum Press, 2003.

SEE ALSO: Achilles; Apocalypse Myths; Dragons; Germanic Peoples; Hel; Loki; Nibelungs; Odin; Scandinavia; Valkyries.

SILENUS

Fat, ugly, constantly drinking wine, and sporting a tail and a pair of horses' ears, Silenus was the guardian and best friend of Dionysus, the Greek god of wine and intoxication. He proved to be a wise and caring companion.

Silenus was a satyr, one of a race of wild male creatures, half human, half animal, who attended Dionysus. The younger satyrs had human heads and chests, with goats' legs, tails, and horns. The older satyrs known as sileni, were more likely to have horses' legs, tails, and ears in addition to human upper bodies. In some stories there were many sileni; in others, Silenus was the only one.

There are various accounts of Silenus's origins. Some relate that he was the son of Pan, god of shepherds and fertility, while other versions say that he was a son of Hermes, messenger of the gods, or Gaia, the ancient earth goddess. Silenus himself was the father of two of the younger satyrs, Astraeus and Maron, and also of a centaur—a creature who was half human, half horse—named Pholus.

Silenus was more powerful than the younger satyrs and was sometimes regarded as a kind of god, although in his appearance and fondness for overindulging he was more like a human. He was usually depicted as a smiling, bald old man with a huge belly, a beard, and a short, stubby nose. He always carried wine with him and was almost always drunk. He often rode a donkey.

Right: This is a classical bust of Silenus. The satyr was famed for his disreputable behavior but also for his wisdom and kindliness.

He was also, however, very wise, and he possessed the ability to predict the future. Yet Silenus was reluctant to act as a seer and was much happier simply enjoying himself. If humans wished the satyr to share his knowledge with them, they had to catch him while he was drunk and tie him up with flowers.

Another aspect of Silenus's character was his caring nature, which he demonstrated in his relationship with Dionysus. Dionysus was the son of Zeus and the mortal Semele. Semele died while pregnant with Dionysus. Zeus snatched the baby from her womb and concealed him in his thigh before giving birth to Dionysus himself. Hera, Zeus's wife, was jealous of her husband's affair and consequently hated the baby. Silenus claimed that he had rescued Dionysus and looked after him so as to protect him from Hera's anger. Later, the satyr became Dionysus's tutor. He taught him how to make wine from grapes and how to keep bees. When the god grew up, Silenus became his most trusted companion. Along with the other satyrs, he rode into battle with Dionysus when the Olympian gods went to war against the Giants.

Myths about Silenus

The best-known myth about Silenus involved Midas, a king of Phrygia in western Asia. According to one version, the drunken Silenus lost his way and became separated from Dionysus and the other satyrs. He came to the beautiful gardens of King Midas, who invited him to stay and threw a great feast in his honor. When Dionysus found Silenus, he was so grateful to the king that he granted him his wish: he wanted to be able to turn anything into gold by touching it—Midas's famous "golden touch." However, in another version, Midas

Above: The Drunken Silenus *by French artist Honoré Daumier (1808–1879). This charcoal drawing depicts Silenus as an inebriated and overweight old man, supported by other satyrs and his donkey.*

trapped the satyr by filling a spring in his garden with wine. Silenus was tempted by this bait, and Midas caught him. Forced to reveal his wisdom in exchange for his freedom, Silenus told Midas that humans are happiest if they are never born, and if they are born, happiest if they die young.

In *Cyclops*, a play by Greek dramatist Euripides (c. 486–c. 406 BCE), Silenus is portrayed as a servant of the Cyclops Polyphemus, the one-eyed giant whom Odysseus encountered on his journey home from the Trojan War. Euripides explained that while pursuing robbers who had kidnapped Dionysus, the ship carrying Silenus and his sons was blown off course in the direction of Polyphemus's island, where they were captured by the Cyclops, and made to serve him. *Cyclops* is a type of play known as a satyr, a comedy that includes a chorus—characters who chant, dance, and comment on the action—of satyrs.

Interpreting Silenus

Like all the satyrs, Silenus represented sensual pleasure and self-indulgence. However, he was a satyr with a difference: he was the only one to be named, and he was older and wiser than the rest of his kind. As a result, despite his drunkenness and ugly appearance, the ancient Greeks regarded him with love and respect. He appeared in a number of satyr plays, as well as in carvings and vase paintings. In ancient Athens people used storage boxes carved into the shape of Silenus. Some Greeks believed that the satyr had invented the flute, or even music itself.

The Greeks also linked Silenus with Athenian philosopher Socrates (c. 470–399 BCE). Like Silenus, Socrates was renowned for an outer ugliness that concealed great inner wisdom. Because of this connection, pictures of Socrates and Silenus often look similar.

The character of a drunken but lovable old man has featured in many works of literature throughout history. One of the most famous examples is Falstaff, a fat, drunken, yet much-loved character who appears in several plays by William Shakespeare. Some scholars think that Shakespeare, who often looked to the classical era for his source material, may have based his character on Silenus.

ANNA CLAYBOURNE

Bibliography

Euripides, and Paul Roche, trans. *10 Plays.* New York: Signet Classic, 1998.

Homer, and Robert Fagles, trans. *The Odyssey.* New York: Penguin USA, 1999.

Howatson, M. C., and Ian Chilvers. *Concise Oxford Companion to Classical Literature.* New York: Oxford University Press, 1993.

SEE ALSO: Cyclopes; Dionysus; Midas; Odysseus; Pan; Satyrs.

SISYPHUS

In Greek mythology, Sisyphus was
known as the most cunning of men.
He ruled the great city of Corinth,
but was also guilty of many crimes,
for which he was punished after
death by a never-ending torment.

Sisyphus was the son of Aeolus and his wife Enarete.
In some versions this was the same Aeolus who was
the god of the winds; in others, Sisyphus's father was
a different Aeolus, the king of Thessaly in northeast Greece.

Sisyphus was a complex character. He was renowned for
his cunning and wisdom, and was a successful leader who
founded the Isthmian Games, an athletics festival held
every two years near Corinth. Yet many of the tales about
Sisyphus reveal a selfish and unpleasant person—a thief
and a trickster who raped or seduced women and attacked
and murdered travelers.

Violent affairs

Sisyphus's wife Merope was one of the Pleiades, the seven
daughters of the Titan Atlas who were later turned into
stars. The giant hunter Orion had wanted to marry
Merope, but instead she chose Sisyphus. Some accounts tell
how Merope was humiliated to be the only one of her
sisters who had married a mortal and that, as a result, her
star was the dullest of all the Pleiades since she hid her face
in shame. With Merope, Sisyphus had four sons, including
Glaucus, who became the father of the hero Bellerophon.

Sisyphus had affairs with a number of other women.
One affair was with his niece Tyro, the daughter of his
brother Salmoneus, whom he hated. Sisyphus learned from
an oracle that if Tyro bore him children, they would kill
Salmoneus. In some versions of the story Sisyphus married

his niece; in others, he raped her. Either way, Tyro and
Sisyphus had two sons. To stop the prophecy from coming
true Tyro killed her children, but her act was in vain: Zeus,
angry at Salmoneus for considering himself the god's equal,
struck him dead with a thunderbolt.

Another story about Sisyphus tells how his cattle were
stolen by Autolycus, a famous thief. The cunning Sisyphus
aimed to catch the culprit red-handed: he fastened lead
tablets, imprinted with the words "stolen by Autolycus," to
his beasts' hooves, and then followed their tracks when they
went missing. In revenge he seduced—or in some versions
raped—Autolycus's daughter Anticlia. Anticlia later gave
birth to the hero Odysseus, whom many believed was the
son of Sisyphus, and not of Anticlia's husband Laertes. This
alternative account of Odysseus's parentage would help
explain the Greek hero's own cunning and ruthless nature.

Right: Sisyphus *by Italian artist Titian (c. 1488–1576). The
painting depicts Sisyphus pushing a heavy boulder up a steep hill—
a never-ending task set as a punishment by the gods, since the boulder
always rolled back down to the bottom again.*

Above: The ruins of Corinth, including this Temple of Apollo, date to the sixth century BCE. Sisyphus was believed to have founded the city.

Founding a city and cheating death

Corinth, on the Greek mainland near Athens, was a powerful city in ancient Greece whose ruins can still be seen today. Some sources relate how Sisyphus founded a great city called Ephyra, later renamed Corinth. Other accounts mention that the enchantress Medea gave Corinth to Sisyphus, who became its king.

One myth tells how Sisyphus gained a source of clean water for his city by making a deal with the river god Asopus. In return for information about Asopus's daughter Aegina, whom Sisyphus had witnessed being abducted by Zeus, the river deity granted him a freshwater spring. Zeus was furious when he learned of this tale-telling and sent Thanatos, the personification of death, to take Sisyphus's life. However, Sisyphus managed to trap Thanatos and imprison him in a dungeon. This imprisonment had a dramatic effect: death could not come for anyone, and so people stopped dying. In response, the gods dispatched Ares, god of war, to rescue Thanatos, who was once again sent to claim Sisyphus. This time, Sisyphus did die, but first he told Merope not to bury him properly. The lack of correct funeral procedure so appalled Hades, lord of the underworld, that he made Sisyphus return to the living to ensure that things were done properly. Once again, Sisyphus had proved his cunning: he refused to go back to the underworld and lived for many more years on earth.

When Sisyphus finally died, Zeus and the other gods devised a terrible punishment for his trickery. He had to push an enormous boulder up a high, steep hill. Every time he neared the top, the boulder rolled down, and Sisyphus had to start again. This torment, the best-known aspect of the Sisyphus myth, was to continue for all eternity.

Symbolism and art

Some scholars have suggested that Sisyphus's punishment has a symbolic meaning. One interpretation is that the boulder represents the sun as it rises and falls each day; another is that it symbolizes humanity's struggle in the endless pursuit of knowledge. Today, the word *sisyphean* describes something that is endless, repetitive, or pointless.

Sisyphus's task captured the imagination of ancient Greek artists, who often depicted it on vases. It has also inspired modern artists, as well as the French writer Albert Camus (1913–1960), whose essay "The Myth of Sisyphus" interpreted the punishment as a symbol for the absurdity of life. Camus concluded that humans can achieve happiness by recognizing this absurdity and rising above it.

ANNA CLAYBOURNE

Bibliography

Camus, Albert, and Justin O'Brien, trans. *The Myth of Sisyphus.* London: Penguin, 2000.
Homer, and Robert Fagles, trans. *The Odyssey.* New York: Penguin USA, 1999.

SEE ALSO: Atlas; Bellerophon; Hades; Odysseus; Pleiades.

SKY

The sky, with all it contains—the sun, moon, stars, rain, wind, and other natural phenomena—has long held a powerful sway on people's imaginations. This influence is reflected in myths from around the world; none more so than the widespread belief that the sky was the home of the gods.

Belief in deities who live in the sky reflects the feeling that many ancient peoples must have had when they looked upward: that the sky's immensity contrasted greatly with the tiny figures of humans walking upon the earth. This feeling of awe helps explain why many cultures believed that their most important gods—creator deities, heads of pantheons, or both—lived in the sky. It also provides a reason for the near universal associations of height with power and moral strength; associations that persist today with words and phrases such as *superior, uplifting,* and *high-minded.*

Another reason for the prominence of the sky in mythology is that it contains and provides so many things crucial for life on earth. These include the sun, which provides light and warmth, and the moon and the stars, which give light at nighttime. The moon also controls the tides of the ocean, while the stars traditionally helped those traveling by sea or by land find their bearings. In addition to these celestial bodies, the sky also provides rain, which fertilizes the soil for plants and swells lakes and rivers with fresh drinking water; and it holds wind, the breath of life itself.

Characteristics of sky deities

Two characteristics shared by sky gods in a range of ancient cultures are the ability to be all-seeing and all-knowing and a responsibility for cosmic law and order. The first quality is a direct result of the sky god's position above the world,

Below: The constantly changing nature of the sky was one reason for the fascination it held for ancient peoples. Another was the importance of the sky—the home of the sun, wind, and rain—to life on Earth.

Paradise in the Sky

Many ancient peoples believed that, after death, those who had lived moral lives ascended to a paradise in the sky. For instance, in the third millennium BCE it was believed that the pharaohs of Egypt would join the sun god Re and serve him on his journeys through the sky. In the ancient Vedic religion of India, people who had lived good lives were thought to join Yama, the god of the dead, in a light-filled place beyond the visible sky. Once there the righteous dead enjoyed such pleasures as music, sexual happiness, and plentiful food and drink. In contrast, the ancient Greeks and Romans believed that the worthy dead went to Elysium, a paradise situated at the end of the earth. However, the concept of ascending to heaven was not entirely unfamiliar, at least to the Romans. According to myth Romulus, the founder of Rome, was caught up in a violent thunderstorm. As the storm raged, he was enveloped in a cloud that was so thick he vanished from sight, never to be seen again. The Romans believed that he had been taken up to heaven by Jupiter.

from where the deity can observe the affairs of and see into the hearts and minds of mortals as well as of lesser gods and goddesses. The second quality reflects the way the sky provides order and regularity for life on earth: the passage from day into night and back again, and the changing of the seasons, from which humans have been able to tell the time and construct calendars. These natural events indicated to ancient peoples that, while their lives may have appeared random and chaotic, the universe was in fact controlled by a higher sense of order.

Some cultures, those for whom their sky god was also their creator god, portrayed a detached figure who was distanced from the affairs of humankind. Myths of this kind commonly reveal a deity who set life on earth in motion but then retreated far away into the heavens. For example, the Ashanti of Ghana, western Africa, believed in a great sky god who used to live close to the earth but then moved away into the farthest reaches of the sky. While the Ashanti felt that they could contact this god by speaking to the wind, there were no rituals associated with him; instead, religious practices centered around other, lesser deities. A similar story was told of Puluga, the supreme sky god of the Andaman Islanders in the Indian Ocean. Puluga created humankind, but after their perpetual misconduct he went away and was never seen again. One suggestion for these myths is that they reflect how—traditionally—the sky was far away and unreachable.

*Right:
A relief
carving
(c. 0–250 CE)
shows the
Mayan sky god
Itzamna seated
on a throne and
holding a serpent.*

Contrasting sky gods

Many mythologies have a range of sky gods who controlled aspects of the weather or celestial bodies. The Maya of ancient Mexico and Central America, for instance, had a thunder god, Ah Peku; a wind god, Huracan; a rain god, Xib Chac; and a god associated with the sun and day and night, Itzamna. The ancient Greeks had an equally complex pantheon, including sky deities such as Helios, the sun; Selene, the moon; Zeus, the chief god, who controlled thunder, lightning, and rain; and the north, south, east, and west winds: Boreas, Notus, Eurus, and Zephyrus, respectively.

Right: This painting, which dates from the early 20th century, depicts the Black Emperor, who in Chinese myth ruled the northern sky. Many ancient cultures had a range of different sky deities.

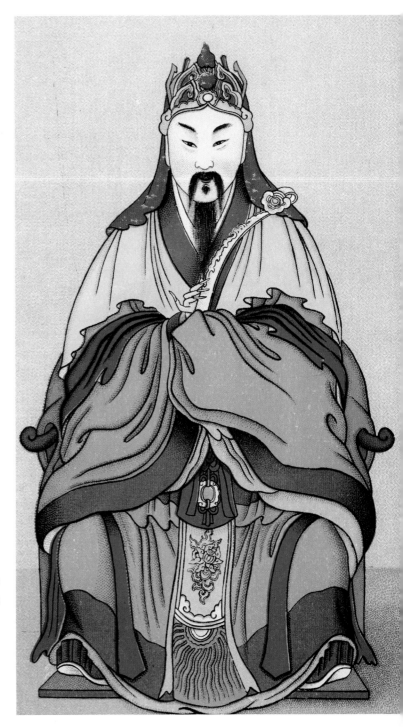

The personalities of sky gods could vary as much as the forces they controlled. In Norse mythology, for example, the supreme sky god Odin was portrayed as wise, cunning, and subtle, while the thunder god Thor was a hasty, angry god of immense strength. Unlike Odin, however, Thor was reliable and was worshiped by ordinary people as the protector of gods and humans against evil.

The Navajo of southwest North America personified their storm gods as several distinct deities. These characters developed conflicts among themselves, especially between Dark Thunder and jealous, bad-tempered Winter Thunder. However, the greatest of the thunders and winds cooperated in teaching humans rituals, which they then used to placate the less evolved, and more erratic, storm gods. Consequently the Navajo believed in both a first realm in the sky, where the better-known Winds and Thunders lived, and a second, higher realm, which was inhabited by the most powerful storm elements.

Indo-European sky gods

Scholars believe that, in some parts of the world, the first deities to be worshiped lived in the earth rather than the sky. In Neolithic Europe (c. 9000–c. 3000 BCE), for example, there is evidence for the worship of earth goddesses—female deities who provided humans with nourishment. Yet by the second millennium BCE, large parts of Europe and northern India had begun to recognize the supremacy of sky gods, the result of a series of invasions by Indo-European-speaking peoples. Historians think that these peoples originally came from the steppes that lie to the north and east of the Caspian Sea. They then moved into central Asia and, between 1900 and 1500 BCE, migrated west to northern Europe and the Mediterranean, and east to Iran and northern India.

Evidence from ancient Greece demonstrates how this change of beliefs occurred. The earliest inhabitants of Greece, the Pelasgians, worshiped an earth-mother figure that reflected the centrality of agriculture to their lives. In contrast, the Indo-European settlers, who in Greece included the Achaeans and the Dorians, brought with them a pantheon of sky gods, of whom Zeus was the chief. The new arrivals mingled their beliefs with those that already existed in their new home. Just as the settlers made cloud-capped Mount Olympus, in northeast Greece, the home of their sky gods, so too they incorporated aspects of the earth goddess to their mythology. Rhea, the Pelasgians' name for the earth goddess, was acknowledged as the mother of Zeus, the Indo-European sky god. Furthermore, while Zeus's realm was undoubtedly that of the sky, his birthplace was on earth, in a cave on Mount Dicte in Crete. And while the sky gods became the dominant figures in Greek myth, a number of stories reveal the age-old importance of the earth goddess. For example, in the myth of the fertility goddess Demeter—arguably another name for the great mother goddess herself—the deity caused the earth to become barren in her sorrow at the loss of her daughter, Persephone. Only when mother and daughter were reunited did the earth flourish again.

A shared Indo-European influence resulted in clear parallels between the chief sky gods of ancient Greece and Rome and India. All personified the sky, all were fathers of gods and mortals, and all used thunder and lightning as their weapons. In ancient Greece, Zeus was the supreme ruler; his authority encompassed law and justice, the defense of the household and property, fertility, and the welfare of humankind in general. In addition, Zeus was a weather god: he produced rain, hail, snow, and thunderstorms. Greek poet Homer (c. ninth–eighth century BCE) attested to these attributes in his epic works the *Iliad* and the *Odyssey*. He referred to Zeus, variously, as "thunderer on high," "cloud gatherer," and "lord of the lightning." Jupiter was the Roman equivalent of Zeus. His temple, which stood on the Capitoline Hill in Rome, was open to the sky in acknowledgment of the god's control over it. Roman priests known as augurs interpreted thunder, lightning, and the flight of birds as signs of Jupiter's intentions.

The Indian sky god Dyaus, however, took on an increasingly remote position in the pantheon. Consequently other sky gods had dominant roles in ancient Indian mythology. The god Indra, for example, ruled the atmosphere between heaven and earth. He fought demons, sent huge rains down upon the earth, and with his thousand testicles made humans, animals, and the land fertile. Another sky god, Varuna, was also capable of sending storms. His main attribute, however, was his ability to see and know all things, while his chief responsibility was for cosmic law and order.

Sky gods in Egypt and western Asia

In contrast to many other cultures, the ancient Egyptians personified the sky as female and the earth as male. In myth, Nut (Sky) married Geb (Earth). All was well until Nut gave birth to four children at once: Isis, Osiris, Nepthys, and Seth. Nut's grandfather Atum, who had begun the process of creation by enjoying the

wonders of his body in total solitude, felt as a result that the world was getting too noisy and crowded. He ordered his son Shu, the god of air, to separate Nut from Geb. Shu moved between the pair and became the atmosphere separating earth from sky. In her new position, Nut, her body spangled with stars, arched over Geb. The only point of contact between her and her husband were the goddess's hands and feet.

While Nut personified the sky, the main Egyptian sky deity was Horus, who was depicted as a falcon whose eyes were said to be the sun and the moon. The Egyptians believed that Horus was the son of the mother goddess Isis and the god of fertility (and, once reincarnated, the god of death) Osiris. According to myth, after Osiris's murder at the hands of his brother Seth, Horus avenged his father by defeating Seth in battle.

In ancient Canaan (which comprised parts of present-day Syria and Palestine) and Mesopotamia (present-day Iraq, northern Syria, and southern Turkey), there were traditions of supreme, if remote, sky gods, and other sky deities who effectively ruled on their behalf. In Canaan, El, the father of the gods, remained in the background, while Baal, the god of storms and rain, had a highly active role.

Right: An Egyptian stela (c. 945–735 BCE) depicts a woman worshiping the god Aten (left). The scene is framed by the arching figure of Nut, the female personification of the sky.

Rainbows

Rainbows have always had a special claim on people's imaginations. In ancient Greece the goddess Iris personified the rainbow. One of Iris's roles was to collect water from the underworld Styx River, which the Olympian gods used to swear solemn oaths. This myth explained the existence of rainbows for the ancient Greeks: they envisaged Iris creating a bridge from the dark, brooding river up to the heavens, along which she carried the icy water in a golden jug. There were diverse beliefs about rainbows in other cultures. The Romans believed that rainbows brought the blessing of Juno, Jupiter's wife. The Babylonians believed that the rainbow was the necklace of Ishtar, goddess of love and fertility. For the Norse, the rainbow was a bridge, Bifröst, linking the world of humans, Midgard, with the home of the gods, Asgard. For the Navajo the rainbow was the goddess Natseelit, whose depiction encircled every sandpainting and had the ability both to protect and to heal.

Right: A rainbow, formed by sunlight falling upon water droplets in the air. Many cultures have regarded rainbows as a sign from the gods.

Baal defeated the sea deity Yam, and as a result proclaimed himself king. Baal became so proud that he challenged Mot, the god of death, but died in the process. However, unlike most sky gods, Baal rose again; a myth that explains why the Canaanites venerated him as the god of the falling rain as well as the growing crops.

In Mesopotamian myth, the supreme god Anu never descended to earth and had little involvement in the affairs of humankind, preferring to stay in the heavens and look after the fate of the universe. His power over mortals was exercised by Enlil, the god of hurricanes. In myth, Enlil became so enraged at the noise made by humans that he sent a huge flood to wipe people from the earth. Like a number of other flood stories, including the account in the Judeo-Christian Bible, only one family and earth's animals survived. Enlil's name in Sumerian meant "lord of the wind," and the god was associated with extremely violent weather. When the city of Ur in southern Mesopotamia was attacked by invaders, the raid was likened to a storm mounted by Enlil.

Sky, wind, and air

Humankind's most immediate connection to the sky is air, whether still or moving as wind. Wind itself has long been a source of fascination. Many ancient cultures regarded it as the breath of life; some also viewed it as a procreative spirit.

Among the Navajo of North America, for example, when First Man and First Woman were created, Wind blew upon their inert forms and quickened them into life, shaping their fingertips, toes, and the crowns of their heads. According to British classical scholar Robert Graves (1895–1985), a Pelasgian creation myth from ancient Greece told how Eurynome, the goddess of all things, set the north wind in motion by her dancing. She caught hold of the wind and rubbed it between her hands until it took on the shape of a serpent named Ophion, with whom she mated. This account may be linked with the Greek and Roman belief in the fertility of Boreas, the north wind. In myth, Boreas took the shape of a dark stallion and fertilized a dozen prized mares. The mares' offspring were so light-footed they could race over a wheat field without bending a single stalk, or run over the sea without making a ripple. Homer wrote that the north wind could inseminate mares if they turned their hindquarters to him; many Greeks and Romans also believed that ancestors were reincarnated as infants—they returned in the form of gusts of wind and entered a woman's womb.

Winds also helped defeat the forces of evil and prepared the land for human habitation. In Mesopotamian myth, the sun god Shamash provided the hero Gilgamesh with winds to use as weapons against the monster Khumbaba. According to the Navajo, the four maternal grandfathers

Greek Winds and War

The ancient Greeks believed that winds had the power to influence the outcome of battles for good and ill. Greek historian Herodotus (c. 484–425 BCE) reported that in 480 BCE the people of Athens called on the assistance of Boreas, the north wind, when a Persian fleet threatened to attack. Violent winds scattered the Persians' ships and defeated their plans to invade. Herodotus urged caution in his account: he was not sure that the wind had come as a result of the Athenians' prayers, but wrote that the citizens believed this to be

Below: This 16th-century painting depicts a storm caused by Aeolus, whom Zeus made guardian of the winds. The storm threatened to destroy the ships of the hero Aeneas.

the case and thanked Boreas by building him a shrine on the banks of the Ilissus River.

Winds also played a role in the Trojan War. According to Homer, both Boreas and Zephyrus, the west wind, combined in a sudden attack on the Greek forces, spreading panic among the soldiers so that their "hearts were torn inside their chests." In another incident Boreas further aided the Trojans when he brought Sarpedon, an ally of the Trojan king Priam, back from the dead with his life-giving breath. Zephyrus was also the father of the magical horses Xanthus and Balius, who were given to the Greek hero Achilles. Xanthus, who had the power of speech, warned Achilles that his return to the fighting would bring about his death.

used wind to blow back the primal waters from a small muddy island as the First People emerged from lower worlds, seeking more room.

The four winds

Many cultures personified the north, south, east, and west winds as separate divine forces. The ancient Greeks believed that Boreas, the north wind, originated in Thrace and was

both creative and destructive, bringing good weather but also frost and snow. Similarly Notus, the south wind, had contrasting qualities, providing rain as well as heat for Mediterranean lands. Mist was another of Notus's gifts, which, as Homer noted, is "better than night to thieves." The Norse of Scandinavia ascribed a more sinister quality to the south wind. In the account of Ragnarok, the last battle between the gods and the forces of evil, the south wind would aid the fire giant Surt in setting the world ablaze and destroy the world tree Yggdrasil. In further contrast, the Ket of Siberia associated their goddess Tomam with the warm southern winds. In Ket mythology, as spring approached, Tomam stood on a cliff overlooking Siberia's Yenisey River and waved her arms through the skies. From her voluminous sleeves flew out clouds of birds—geese, swans, and ducks—that rode the southern winds to the north, bringing renewed fertility. In fall these birds migrated back to the goddess.

The Greeks called the east wind Eurus, regarding it as a morning wind that melted snow and brought rains. For the Norse, the east wind also had a role in Ragnarok, propelling the death ship Naglfar, with its crew of the enemies of the gods, toward the battle. According to the poem *Völuspá* (c. 1000 CE), the evil trickster deity Loki would steer this ship from out of the east. The Greeks believed that Zephyrus, their west wind, also had a connection with death—a symbolic one deriving from its nature as an evening wind—but the west wind was also linked to new life. Like Boreas, Zephyrus had the ability to fertilize mares. One myth told how Zephyrus fathered Achilles' immortal horses, Xanthus and Balius, from the

harpy Podarge—one of three winged female monsters (part human, part bird) who were goddesses of the storm winds. Favonius, the Roman equivalent of Zephyrus, was also connected with fresh life: in the Roman calendar February 8 marked the beginning of the period when Favonius would fertilize all creatures and plants.

Myths of the sky people

Many ancient mythologies tell of creator gods who lived in the sky. Some cultures also believed that the first peoples actually inhabited the sky. The Seneca, Iroquois-speaking Native Americans who lived in present-day New York State and Ohio, told how, before the world was made, people lived in a village in the sky. In the middle of the village stood a tree with enormous white flowers, which provided light for the sky people. According to the myth, one of the women in the village was told in a dream that the tree should be uprooted. When she related her dream to the rest of the villagers, they agreed to dig the soil away from the tree's roots, but when the tree sank through a hole and disappeared, everyone became angry with the woman and the chief pushed her through the hole. She fell toward the lower world, which at this point was nothing but water. Her descent was observed by birds who swam on the surface of the water. They took turns diving as far as they could to determine whether the water had a bottom. After a long time one of the birds brought up some earth, which the other animals placed on the back of a turtle to form the ground on which the woman landed.

The Yekuhana of Venezuela also believed in the existence of sky people who predated the emergence of humankind on earth. According to their creation myth, in the beginning there were only sky and light. The first sun to rise initiated the process of creation by blowing on some quartz crystals and forming Wanadi, the creator god and sky deity. Wanadi himself blew on more quartz crystals to make the sky people. The people built homes and villages in the sky, where they lived peacefully without evil, disease, war, or death. There were no animals but plenty of food, and the sky people were happy.

Left: A Pawnee ceremonial drum, depicting Thunderbird, the creator of storms, hurling lightning at swallows. Many Native Americans believed that the first people lived in the sky.

Above: The Navajo considered Monument Valley (pictured here) in the American Southwest to be sacred. Mountains and high plateaus were commonly held to be holy places in ancient cultures because of their proximity to the sky.

Wanadi then decided that people should live on earth as well as in the sky. Again, he blew on some quartz crystals and "Wanadi the Wise" came into existence. Wanadi the Wise left the sky for earth, where he cut his umbilical cord and buried it. He then created earth people by smoking his pipe and dreaming of them. However, he was not fated to be their master: as his umbilical cord rotted it gave birth to the demon Odosha, who tempted the earth people with

Touching the Sky

Mountains have often been regarded as sacred places because they reach up to the sky. According to the ancient Vedic religion of India, mountains strained so hard to touch the sky that they once had wings. In central Asia there was a widespread belief in a world mountain, situated in the far north and rising up to the Pole Star, which was a temple on its peak. This world mountain was the home of the gods, a notion that finds a parallel with Greece's Mount Olympus. Olympus, standing on the border of Macedonia and Thessaly, is the highest mountain in Greece. It was believed to be the home of the gods ruled by Zeus, leading to the description of such deities as "Olympian." Over the centuries the Greeks distinguished between the home of the gods and the mountain, believing that the deities lived in the sky above Mount Olympus.

evil thoughts. Wanadi the Wise punished the people for their wickedness by turning them into animals. His act was not enough, however, and he realized the animals would always be under Odosha's control. So Wanadi the Wise returned to the sky. The creator Wanadi then blew on more crystals and sent his new offspring, Wanadi II, to create new people on earth, but before Wanadi II had brought the race into existence, Odosha tricked Wanadi II's nephew, Iarakaru, into opening Wanadi II's magical bag and letting out darkness, so that night hid the sky from earth.

Wanadi II returned to the sky; in his place, the original Wanadi created Wanadi III, who was also sent down to earth to make a new people. Wanadi III created the sun, moon, and stars so that the people of earth would have light. He created the first humans and provided them with homes and food. The Yekuhana believed, however, that Odosha remained master of the earth, which explained the existence of evil, disease, and death, but they also believed that the demon would, at last, die, causing the sun, moon, and stars to fall out of the sky and the real sky, no longer obscured by darkness, to become visible once more, ushering in a new age of peace and happiness.

KATHLEEN JENKS

Bibliography

Davidson, H. R. Ellis. *Myths and Symbols in Pagan Europe.* Syracuse, NY: Syracuse University Press, 1988.

Reichard, Gladys A. *Navaho Religion: A Study of Symbolism.* Tucson, AZ: University of Arizona Press, 1983.

SEE ALSO: Baal; Creation Myths; Egypt; Enlil; Greece; Helios; Horus; India; Jupiter; Maya; Mesopotamia; Moon; Native Americans; Natural Forces; Scandinavia; Stars; Sun; Zeus.

SLAVS

Since the first century CE, Slavs have been the largest group of European peoples sharing common ethnic and linguistic roots. Originally Slavs migrated to Europe from Asia. Archaeologists think the Lusatian culture of northern Germany, which dates from the second millennium BCE, was Slavic. Some scholars believe that the earliest written reference to Slavs occurs in the work of Greek historian Herodotus (c. 484–425 BCE).

Slavs who settled in eastern and southeastern Europe were an ethnolinguistic group which, by the fifth century CE, had divided into three blocs: Antae, or East Slavs, comprising Belarusians, Russians, and Ukrainians; Sklaveni, or South Slavs (Bosnians, Bulgarians, Croats, Macedonians, Montenegrins, Serbs, and Slovenes); and Venedi, or West Slavs (Czechs, Poles, Slovaks, and the Wends of eastern Germany).

Modern knowledge of early Slavic religion is sketchy at best, and it is unsafe to use what little evidence there is to generalize about such a varied and widely distributed ethnic grouping. However, before the rise of Christianity and Islam, it appears that most Slavic peoples believed in animism and magic. They revered the four elements—Fire, Water, Sky, and Earth—and commonly divided them into two dualistic pairs. Fire demanded respect; it was

Below: This 15th-century painting from a convent in Dubrovnik, Croatia, depicts Saint Blaise and Saint Paul. In many areas, Christianity replaced traditional Slavic ancestor worship with the iconography of saints.

The Slavic Blocs c. 550–c. 1200 CE

GERMANY

POLAND

BELARUS

RUSSIA

UKRAINE

BALKAN
STATES

BLACK SEA

TURKEY

East Slavs

West Slavs

South Slavs

| 0 | 500 miles |
| 0 | 805 km |

sacrilege to spit into a fire. Water, symbol of life and death, commanded reverence; the Dnieper and Volga rivers were scenes of human and animal sacrifices. Sky was personified by winds known as the grandchildren of Stribog (god of air, sky, weather, and wind). Mountains and trees were sacred because that is where Sky and Earth met; so, for a similar reason, were lightning and thunder. Earth—known as Mati Syra Zemlja ("Mother Moist Earth")—was highly respected; hoeing could not begin until after Maslenica (the spring equinox), because, until then, the earth was regarded as pregnant. Oaths were sworn while holding pieces of earth. Brides and grooms recited wedding vows with clumps of soil in their mouths or on their heads. When holy men were unavailable, sins were confessed directly to the earth; people sought forgiveness for their sins from the earth when they were preparing to die.

Deities

According to one of the most widespread Slavic myths, the earth was created when an unnamed creator god ordered that a handful of sand be brought up from the seabed. In most versions of the legend, it was the devil who brought it; in a few, it was the god himself. Although 12th-century Christian missionaries in the region expressed surprise that

Some Important Slav Deities

Baba Yaga:	Thunder witch.
Belobog:	White god; deity of happiness and luck.
Chernobog:	Black god; deity of evil, grief, and woe.
Dazhdebog:	God of gifts; ancestor of Russian people.
Div:	Once god of the sky; became woodland deity after his overthrow by Perun.
Dodol:	Goddess of air, clouds, and rain.
Dolya:	Goddess of happiness and luck.
Khors:	God of sun and light.
Kostroma:	Fertility goddess, personification of spring.
Kruchina:	Goddess of mourning.
Lada:	Goddess of love and beauty.
Marena:	Goddess of winter, hunger, and death.
Nav:	Goddess of death.
Perun:	God of lightning, thunder, and war.
Semargl:	Seven-headed god of soil and fertility.
Stribog:	God of air, sky, weather, and wind.
Troyan:	Three-headed god of night and darkness.
Ustrecha:	Goddess of happiness and luck.
Zhiva:	Goddess of vigor; chief deity of West Slavs.

Creation Myth: Land and the Sweetness of Honey

One Slav creation myth describes the relationship between the good white god Belobog and the evil black god Chernobog. In the beginning there was only primordial sea, and Belobog and Chernobog fought each other for it. Together, they created land, and Belobog controlled it. However, he could not stop it from growing, and it began to cover too much of the earth; only Chernobog knew how to stop it from spreading. Belobog sent a bee to discover the secret. The bee heard Chernobog say to a goat, "Stupid Belobog! The secret is to cross two sticks to the four points of the compass and say 'That is enough earth!'" The bee buzzed off in excitement; Chernobog yelled after the bee, "Let whoever sent you eat your excrement!" The bee told Belobog what Chernobog had said. Using the crossed sticks, Belobog stopped the earth from growing, and then said to the bee: "Let no excrement taste sweeter than yours." Thus Slavs explained both the creation of the world and the sweetness of honey.

the indigenous population already believed in a single heavenly god, other evidence suggests that this was an oversimplification of a more complex cosmology. This one god took no interest in the world or in human affairs, and other deities filled the gap. For example, ancient inhabitants of Bosnia, Poland, and Slovenia believed that their wooden homes were inhabited by the spirits of the trees from which their houses had been built. These minor deities could be good or malignant. More commonly, early Slavs seem to have believed in two main gods, one black, the other white. Although nearly every early Slavic people had a god of thunder and lightning, he was normally simply that—there was no idea, as in other cultures, that the master of these natural forces was supreme or omnipotent.

Below: This 20th-century Russian charcoal drawing depicts one of the tree spirits that were believed to inhabit wooden houses.

In Belarus, there was a supreme being who was manifested in four forms, each of which was dedicated to bringing sustenance to the people. They were *bog* ("god"), *sporysh* (an edible herb or stalk of grain, a symbol of abundance), *ray* ("paradise"), and *dobro* ("good").

Moon worship

Of all celestial bodies, the moon was most highly venerated, above even the sun. Ukrainians believed that life would be insupportable without it. In Slavic languages the moon is masculine, and often described as "father," "brother," or "uncle." According to one Serbian tradition, humans have a "grandfather" (in other words, a new moon) for every month that they have lived. In some pagan Russian prayers the new moon is addressed as Adam—the forefather of all humans. The feminine sun was sometimes depicted as the moon's bride. It was the moon that, if

Major Agricultural Holidays

Major agricultural holidays involved ritual feasts, songs, and activities. The festival of Koljada celebrated the winter solstice; people paraded wearing masks, sang in return for animal-shaped pastries, and invited ancestral spirits inside to warm themselves. Strinennia, signaling spring, was held on March 9; bird-shaped pastries were tossed into the air by children who shouted, "The birds have come." Maslenica celebrated the spring equinox with horse races, boxing, and mock battles. Farms were encircled with religious icons or brooms; "sweeping" created a magic circle against evil. Many ancient Slav festivals were later linked to Christian dates. Originally known as Nav Dien (Day of the Dead), Radunica, on the second Tuesday after Easter, celebrated ancestors with cemetery feasts: food was left out for the dead. St. Egorij Day was April 23, the day flocks were driven into the fields. Rusal'naia Week was celebrated the seventh or eighth week after Easter, when Rusalki (female water-spirits) went from rivers into forests. Girls placed fried eggs and beer under trees. Kupalo was a celebration of the summer solstice, with baths taken as the morning sun appeared above the horizon. Fire rituals dominated Kupalo: fires were ritually extinguished and rekindled, scarecrow effigies were burned, and bonfires ensured fertility: couples jumped over them, and cattle were driven through their flames. Perun's Day was July 20: a human sacrifice, chosen by ballot, kept Perun from sending late-summer storms to destroy crops. After August 2, harvest celebrations were functional: until the autumn equinox, work parties went from farm to farm, singing ritual songs as they gathered in the harvest.

correctly propitiated, would provide health and abundance. Early Slavs believed that lunar eclipses were attempts by a monster to devour the moon, so during such events they fired missiles into the sky in an effort to scare it off.

Sacred places and holy days

Ancient Slav places of worship were often built in triangles of land at the confluence of rivers. They were surrounded by fortified enclosures. Within these structures were effigies of gods made of wood, metal, or combinations of both. These deities were always broadly human in form, but they often had extra body parts—as many as seven arms and five heads. The whole population of the surrounding district would gather at these shrines once a year to slaughter their oxen or sheep. It was here, too, that human sacrifices—typically decapitations or disembowelings—were performed to ensure good harvests or military victories.

Some of the gods depicted in the shrines were founders of the local clan. A single effigy might represent more than one such ancestor, thus explaining the many limbs and faces of some votive statues. Feasts held at the shrine annually or as often as four times a year commemorated these ancestral spirits, and people took advantage of these occasions to hold markets and festivals. In Russia, such traditions survived into the 20th century.

Below: This painting by Grigory Myasoyedov (1834–1911) depicts harvest time in Russia. Many early Slavic festivals coincided with key dates in the agricultural calendar.

Right: This 1902 color lithograph depicts Baba Yaga, the ancient Slavic thunder witch. Russian parents still threaten children that Baba Yaga will come and eat them if they are naughty.

In the Balkans, especially in lands along the banks of the Danube River, Slavs customarily reopened the graves of their ancestors every three, five, or seven years, washed the corpses, wound them in fresh linen, and reinterred them. The festival of Koljada was an annual visit made by the spirits of the dead, disguised as beggars, to all the houses in the village. At Krivichi (a region of modern Belarus) archaeologists have discovered burial mounds containing the ashes of large numbers of people who seem to have all been cremated at one time. Similar prehistoric earthworks have been found at Kurgan, a city of Russia on the Tobol River, east of the Ural Mountains in western Siberia. Some Slavic peoples memorialized their dead by lighting ceremonial fires from time to time on top of their graves—while the exact symbolism of such acts is obscure, the practice persisted into modern times.

The unclean and the undead

The early Slavs' preoccupation with ancestor worship was matched by their concerns about the nature of physical decomposition after death. There is evidence that some Slavic peoples kept the bones of their dead relatives in a special corner of their homes—this practice was superseded by the Christian icons that modern Orthodox families erect in their dwellings.

The spirits of people who lived long lives, had children, and died naturally, were venerated. The spirits of those who were prematurely deprived of life, however, were greatly feared, because it was believed that they would want to come back and steal from the living the joys that would have been theirs if they had not been cut off. They are the so-called unclean dead. Slavs were particularly afraid of maidens who died before they could marry—they were thought to come out at night in search of living bridegrooms and babies, whom they would kidnap to the grave. One annual festival in particular, the Semik (seventh Thursday after Easter), was dedicated to the expulsion of these spirits.

The bodies of people who had died before their time might not decompose in their graves. Instead, they might become the undead, or vampires—both the English word *vampire* and the concept of vampirism are of Slavic origin. In order to prevent the vampire from rising to feed from the blood of the living, it was necessary either to drive a stake through the heart of the body as it lay in the grave, or to exhume the corpse and burn it.

This ancient Slavic superstition was widely disseminated by Christians—inadvertently, because early church missionaries intended to allay pagan fears of this nature. More recently vampirism was popularized worldwide, first by *Dracula*, a novel by Irishman Bram Stoker (1847–1912), and later by numerous movie versions of the legend. Among many modern embellishments of the original story is the idea that vampires cower at the sight of a crucifix—Slavs almost certainly believed in vampires more than a millennium before the birth of Jesus.

ALYS CAVINESS

Bibliography
Franklin, Anna. *The Illustrated Encyclopaedia of Fairies.* London: Vega, 2002.
Gimbutas, Marija A. *The Goddesses and Gods of Old Europe.* Berkeley, CA: University of California Press, 1982.
Hudec, Ivan, Dusan Caplovic, and Emma Nezinska, trans. *Tales from Slavic Myths.* Wauconda, IL: Bolchazy Carducci, 2001.
Phillips, Charles, and Michael Kerrigan. *Forests of the Vampires: Slavic Myth (Myth and Mankind).* New York: Time-Life Books, 2000.

SEE ALSO: Ancestor Worship; Animism; Baltic, The; Death and the Afterlife; Moon; Nature Religions; Paganism; Sacrifice.

SOUTHEAST ASIA

Southeast Asia is the huge mainland area and complex of islands that lie east of India and south of China. It includes Cambodia, Indonesia, Laos, Malaysia, Myanmar (Burma), the Philippines, Singapore, Thailand, and Vietnam. The geographical position of Southeast Asia is significant because the religions and cultures of India and China have had a profound impact on the region's beliefs. This is not to say, however, that Southeast Asia passively adopted the religions brought in by traders, missionaries, and colonists. On the contrary, the region's belief systems, pantheons, and myths owe much to the fusion of these outside beliefs with indigenous traditions of creator gods, spirits, demons, and ghosts.

Hinduism first came from India to Southeast Asia around 300 BCE, most likely brought by traders who journeyed to the region in search of spices. The traders were followed by Indian Brahmins, or priests, who converted local chiefs to Hinduism and preached a concept of divine kingship that was to have a significant effect on the region. This concept held that rulers who recognized Siva, the Hindu god of destruction and restoration, took on Siva's physical and spiritual power themselves. Cambodian monarch Jayavarman II (c. 770–850 CE) developed this belief: he declared that a king did not rule by divine authority alone but was a god himself, the incarnation of Siva on Earth. Jayavarman laid the foundations for a civilization that lasted 600 years. To consolidate the cult of divine kings, his successors built angkors (holy cities), in which grand buildings and waterworks attempted to replicate the heavenly home of the Indian gods. The most impressive of these temples were Angkor Wat, built by King Suryavarman II (reigned c. 1113–1150), and Angkor Thom, built by King Jayavarman VII (c. 1120–c. 1215); (see box, page 1324).

Buddhism also had a deep and lasting impact on Southeast Asia. The religion was widespread in India by the third century BCE, but it was not established elsewhere until the first centuries CE, when a resurgence of

Below: The 12th-century temple of Angkor Wat, the world's largest religious building, is an architectural masterpiece.

Right: This statue at the Shwe Dagon Pagoda in Yangon, Myanmar, represents one of the local religion's holy nats, *or spirits.*

Hinduism in India led many Buddhist monks to leave their homeland and settle in Southeast Asia. Buddhism also established itself in China, where it competed with and borrowed from existing religions and the philosophical tradition of Taoism. As a result, Buddhism entered Southeast Asia from both the west and the north, although in two different forms. The teachings of the Buddha introduced a new element of compassion into people's beliefs. For example, a myth from the Indonesian island of Java tells how Hariti, an ancient Indian goddess of infant mortality, converted to Buddhism. Hariti had 500 children of her own, but devoured the children of human mothers. One day, the Buddha caused one of the goddess's own children to disappear. The pain of losing a child led Hariti to adopt Buddhism, and henceforth she refrained from killing any more infants.

Confucianism and Islam

Other beliefs had influences on regions within Southeast Asia. The Chinese political and religious ideas of Confucianism were felt most strongly in Vietnam, the northern part of which belonged to the Chinese Empire between the third century BCE and 906 CE. Chinese beliefs had a lasting impact there: Vietnamese legend held that the country's rulers were descended from Chinese dragon lords. Islam gained a foothold in Indonesia in the late 13th century CE, benefiting from the decline of the islands' Hindu–Buddhist kingdoms as a result of war, famine, and a series of volcanic eruptions. Except for the inhabitants of Bali, most Indonesian peoples converted to the Muslim faith. A myth of the Bada people on the island of Sulawesi reflects this transition: it relates a contest between the god of heaven, Ala Tala, whose name is a variant of Allah, and Wuali, king of the spirits, who was most likely a pre-Muslim deity worshiped by the Bada. In the myth, Wuali challenged Ala Tala to a javelin-throwing competition to determine which of them had the right to rule the earth. While Wuali's javelin soon landed in the ground, Ala Tala's javelin never came to rest, but flew higher and higher into the sky.

The religions introduced to Southeast Asia by traders, colonists, and missionaries mingled with indigenous beliefs to form rich mythologies. Some beliefs were a fusion of different religions that had arrived from elsewhere. For example, before their conversion to Islam, inhabitants of the Indonesian island of Java merged Hinduism and Buddhism.

In his poem *Sutasoma*, 14th-century Javanese poet Tantular wrote: "God Buddha is no different from Siva, the supreme god. Both gods contain all the elements. How can anyone divide that which is essentially one?" This syncretism (merging) of Hinduism and Buddhism occurred in Cambodia, too: the country's angkor-building kings identified themselves not only with Siva but also with the Buddha. Another characteristic of Southeast Asian religion was the merging of these "external" beliefs with the ancient worship of ancestors and spirits. Myanmar has a long tradition of spirit cults that have always existed alongside Buddhism. The most prominent cult in Myanmar is based on the *nats*, spirits of great men or women who

Angkor Wat and Angkor Thom

The enormous temples at Angkor Wat and Angkor Thom in northern Cambodia were attempts by the country's 12th-century kings to demonstrate their power and divine majesty. The temple at Angkor Wat, measuring 5,000 by 4,000 feet (1,500 by 1,200 m), remains the largest religious building in the world. Every detail of this vast structure reproduces the heaven of Hindu mythology. The highest tower in the temple represents the heavenly summit of Mount Meru, home of the gods. The other four towers depict the mountains surrounding this central peak, while the moat represents the ocean. Bas-relief sculptures on the temple walls show scenes from Indian epics *Mahabharata* and *Ramayana*, together with images of Hindu gods Brahma, Vishnu, and Siva, and the temple's founder, King Suryavarman II (ruled c. 1113–1150 CE).

Angkor Thom, founded by King Jayavarman VII (ruled 1181–c. 1215 CE), was also laid out according to a sacred design. Stone walls replicate a great serpent over which the gods of heaven fought with the deities of the underworld in order to obtain the liquor of immortality it contained. The central temple at Angkor Thom, the Bayon, also represents a heavenly mountain, while each of the temple's 50 towers depicts four images of Jayavarman himself, looking out in all directions.

Left: This photograph shows one of the images of Jayavarman VII on the towers of the temple at Angkor Thom, Cambodia.

suffered violent deaths. Festivals honoring the *nats* are occasions of unrestrained, extravagant behavior. They serve as outlets for people who otherwise try to lead the calm, ordered lifestyle prescribed by Buddhism.

Major deities in Southeast Asia

The gods and spirits of Southeast Asian mythology reflect both external influences on the region and the region's own rich traditions of beliefs. The peoples of Indonesia have traditionally worshiped a wide range of deities. In Balinese myth, Semara, god of love, lived in the sky, while beneath him the underworld was ruled by the goddess Setesuyara and the god Batara Kala, who also created light and earth. The god Barong, king of spirits, was believed to lead the forces of good in a series of battles against the demon queen Rangda.

Other Indonesian myths reveal the influence of Hinduism. Before the advent of Islam, peoples of Sumatra worshiped the Hindu god Siva, whom they called Batara Guru. One myth about Batara Guru involved his daughter, Tisna Wati. The girl fell in love with a human farmer, but her father objected to the affair. When he found out that his daughter had disobeyed him and talked to the farmer, Batara Guru changed Tisna Wati and the farmer into stalks of rice. The inhabitants of Java recognized the Hindu creator deity Brahma as their supreme god; one of their other gods was Hanuman, divine monkey chief of Indian mythology, who plays a central role in the Hindu epic *Ramayana*. This work was retold throughout Southeast Asia and had an important influence on the early literature of the region.

Like many Southeast Asian countries, Thailand had an extensive pantheon of gods. The principal deity was Phra In, lord of heaven and god of wealth who, like Siva, possessed a third eye with which he could see everything that humans could not. Phra In saw how humans were suffering because they told too many lies. He sent two

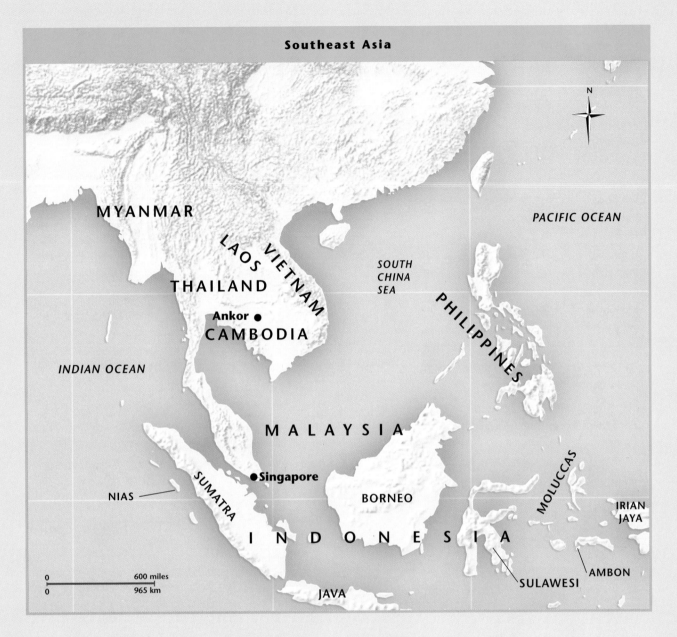

Southeast Asia

MYANMAR

LAOS

VIETNAM

THAILAND

PACIFIC OCEAN

SOUTH
CHINA
SEA

PHILIPPINES

Ankor ●

CAMBODIA

INDIAN OCEAN

MALAYSIA

●Singapore

NIAS

SUMATRA

MOLUCCAS

BORNEO

IRIAN
JAYA

INDONESIA

AMBON

0   600 miles
0   965 km

SULAWESI

JAVA

giants from heaven to erect a sacred pillar that radiated virtue and allowed people to live happier, purer, and more prosperous lives. Eventually, however, the people forgot to honor Phra In and reverted to their old dishonest habits, so the god sent the giants to take the pillar back to heaven. The country soon became poor again.

Phra Sao was the Thai god of fickle fortune, who could bring both good and bad luck. People recognized five signs that indicated whether a person had offended Phra Sao: sweating, paleness, shivering, cloudy vision, and feelings of gloom. These signs were portents of bad luck, which could range from a person's horse breaking its leg to defeat in battle and death. Other Thai deities included the rice goddess Devi Sri and the Thens, three divine beings who, together with the three great men—Pu Lang Seung, Khun K'an, and Khun K'et—established human society.

Other major deities in Southeast Asia included the creator spirits Ara and Irik of Borneo; Kadaklan, the thunder god of the Tinguian people of the Philippines; and Mahatara, supreme god of the Dyak of Borneo. One Malaysian myth told of the hero spirit Moyang Kapir and the half-human, half-tiger spirit Moyang Melur. For a long time the fearsome Moyang Melur, who lived on the moon, kept the rules of civilized human behavior to himself. As a result, humans committed murder, incest, and cannibalism because they knew no better. One night, Moyang Melur was watching the chaos in the world below him but leaned too far out from the moon and fell to Earth, where he encountered Moyang Kapir. Moyang Melur told the hero that unless he returned to the moon immediately, he would kill everyone on Earth. Moyang Kapir responded by throwing a rope to the moon and climbing up it with

Southeast Asian Deities

Name	Status
Ala Tala:	God of heaven (Sulawesi).
Ara and Irik:	Creator spirits (Borneo).
Barong:	Spirit king (Bali).
Batara Guru:	Creator god (Sumatra).
Batara Kala:	Underworld god (Bali).
Brahma:	Creator deity (India).
Burung Une:	Agriculture deity (Borneo).
Devi Sri:	Rice goddess (Thailand).
Hanuman:	Monkey god (Java).
Kadaklan:	Supreme god and thunder god (Philippines).
Mahatara:	Supreme god (Borneo).
Phra In:	God of wealth and creation (Thailand).
Phra Sao:	God of fickle fortune (Thailand).
Po Tlen:	Underworld god (Vietnam).
Rangda:	Demon queen.
Semara:	God of love (Bali).
Setesuyara:	Underworld goddess (Bali).
Thens:	Creator spirits (Thailand and Laos).
Tisna Wati:	Daughter of Batara Guru (Sumatra).
Wuali:	King of spirits (Sulawesi).

Below: These theatrical masks represent Barong and Rangda, personifications of good and evil, for a popular form of dance drama in Bali.

the other spirit. However, just as Moyang Melur was planning to eat Moyang Kapir, the latter escaped back down the rope, taking the bag that contained the rules of civilized behavior. Back on Earth, he taught humans these rules so that they would stop abusing each other.

Creation myths

Southeast Asian mythology contains a rich variety of stories that explain the origins of the world, its people, and natural phenomena. The Dyak of Borneo explained the creation of the world by telling of a spider that descended from heaven by spinning a long web. A piece of coral and a stone then fell from heaven and landed on the web, forming the ground. A slug and a worm fell onto the ground and formed soil. Other objects from heaven fell onto this soil: a sapling, which formed trees; a crab, which dug down into the soil and threw up hills and mountains; and rainwater, which formed lakes and rivers. Next to fall from heaven were two spirits who created a sword handle and a loom, which in turn gave birth to children. After a few generations, the early children of Earth gave birth to a god and goddess of agriculture, Amei Awi and Burung Une. These gods had eight human children, whom they sent to climb a high mountain. The humans who reached the top of the mountain were the ancestors of slaves, since they were strong and capable of hard work. The humans who stopped halfway up the mountain became the ancestors of free men and women, while those who did

not even attempt the climb were the ancestors of kings, who made other people work for them. Amei Awi and Burung Une then withdrew below the surface of the earth, from where they continued to rule all plant life. The Dyak believed that sacrifices and prayers to these two gods were essential to ensure good harvests.

The peoples of Thailand and Laos believed that human society was created by three divine beings known as the Thens, who lived in the upper world. The Thens demanded that all people on Earth should offer them part of their meals before eating. When the people refused to comply, the Thens sent a great flood that wiped out all but three of the people. These three, known as the great men, were allowed to shelter in heaven until the floodwaters subsided. When they returned to Earth, the king of the Thens gave them a buffalo. In time the buffalo died and a plant began to grow from its nostrils. This plant bore three fruits from which a new race of humans emerged. The three great men taught humans the skills of farming and weaving; they were assisted by the Thens, who gave humans the knowledge of telling time, making tools, preparing food, and playing music.

Other Southeast Asian myths explained the origins of natural phenomena. The Badui of Java told a story that explained how volcanoes came into being. In the myth, monkey god Hanuman built a huge fortress out of rocks to protect his monkey subjects from attack by tigers. When the fortress was finished, the monkeys began to behave badly—the fortress was so high that, when they were on its summit, they could take bites out of the stars. Following the orders of the supreme god Brahma, Hanuman had no choice but to cut off the top third of his fortress with a pair of scissors. The piece of rock fell to the earth with such force that it began to smoke. Another Dyak myth from Borneo explained the pockmarked surface of the moon. In addition to their eight human children, the deities Amei Awi and Burung Une produced four lunar children. Full Moon was the most beautiful of these offspring, but her appearance inspired the jealousy of her brother, Crescent Moon. While the four children were eating porridge, Crescent Moon threw some in his sister's face, creating the dark spots on the moon where his sister's face was burned.

Rice myths

Several Southeast Asian myths relate the origin of rice cultivation, reflecting the importance of this staple crop throughout the region. According to one tale from Thailand, the first humans did not have to plant or harvest rice—the crop grew in the fields and, when the grains

Below: According to the creation myth of the Dayak of Borneo, the world was formed by a heavenly spider.

The Mythical Origin of Countries

Some myths of Southeast Asian countries attempt to explain how they were founded. In a legend from Myanmar, for example, one day the Buddha looked out his window and saw a mole emerging from the ground. The mole offered the Buddha some flowers, and the Buddha smiled, knowing that 110 years after he had attained nirvana (enlightenment), the ground on which the mole stood would be a great kingdom and the mole himself would be king.

In Cambodian myth, Prince Thong, leader of the Khmer (Cambodians), brought his people to the region that would become known as Cambodia. On the shore of Lake Anlong Reach the prince fell in love with a half-woman, half-snake spirit, the daughter of a spirit king who ruled the land and the waters. The spirit king approved of the union. In order to give the Khmer people enough land on which to live and farm, he drained a vast amount of the lake by drinking it. Prince Thong's spirit wife became known as Queen of the Waters, and successive Khmer rulers were believed to mate with her in order to ensure that there was always enough water for their subjects' crops.

were ripe, they rolled together to form balls. These rice balls then rolled into people's grain barns, and everyone lived in abundance. This system broke down when some people began to build bigger barns so that they would have more rice than other people, and before long fights broke out over ownership of the crop. The gods punished humans for their greed by taking away all the rice from the earth. However, rice goddess Devi Sri pitied the starving humans. She instructed them that they would have rice again, but only if they began to plant the rice seedlings, weed the fields, harvest the rice, and then thresh it and cook it.

A myth from Sulawesi tells how rice was a gift to humans from Wuali, king of the spirits. Ala Tala, god of heaven and creator of humans, had forbidden Wuali to talk to humans during their first seven days on Earth, adding that they would have to find their own food. Wuali, however, who disputed Ala Tala's rule on Earth, gave the first people the seeds of the rice plant. Ala Tala was offended that Wuali had disobeyed him, but recognized the spirit king's generosity. He declared that rice should be the staple crop of humans.

Below: Rice is the staple crop throughout Southeast Asia, and is hence the subject of numerous myths.

Ancestors, the soul, and the afterlife

Many peoples in Southeast Asia have traditionally believed in the existence of a human soul that survives the death of the body and remains in contact with people on Earth. Beliefs vary about the nature of these souls. The Meo of Vietnam, for instance, believe that a human has three souls, which, after death, enter the womb of a woman to be reborn as a baby. The Kachin of Myanmar believe that all people have a perfect soul known as a *krin*, which after death remains in its family home, where people make offerings to it. This krin can be reborn as a child or a tame animal, such as a cat or a dog. Inhabitants of the Indonesian island of Ambon believe that souls stay near their graves for as long as the graves are kept in decent condition. People regard it as in their best interests to maintain the graves: they believe that the souls of the departed will protect their children and give them messages in their dreams.

Ancestor worship is connected to the belief that the souls of the dead can offer guidance and protection for their descendants. The people of Nias, another island of Indonesia, offer sacrifices to their ancestors. They believe that serious illness is the result of sins against these forebears. Any such wrong may be righted by erecting a new statue to a dead family member. In some Southeast

Above: On the Indonesian island of Sulawesi, eminent people are buried in tree houses such as this. Their spirits are given land to farm.

Asian societies there is a hierarchy of ancestor worship. For example, the Toraja people of Indonesia place worship of heroes who died in battle above those who founded their village. In addition to these spirits are the ancestors of homeowners, who are venerated by the current occupants of the house. Dead souls are usually honored with offerings of food and drink at mealtimes, festivals, and after harvests. Inhabitants of Sulawesi traditionally set aside a small area of land for their ancestors to farm, and they provide the souls with imitation tools. They also plant beans, rice, and yams for the dead to harvest.

There are many different conceptions of the afterlife in Southeast Asian mythology. The Thay of northern Vietnam believe that souls go to the kingdom of the dead, which is ruled by underworld deity Po Tlen. Once there, the souls cultivate rice as they did on the earth. Not every soul makes this journey to the underworld, however. The souls of women and babies who die in childbirth remain on the earth, where special rituals must be performed to prevent them from becoming evil spirits. The Kachin of Myanmar believe that the land of the dead is to the north of their

country, in the direction from which their ancestors originally came. The Kachin regard this otherworld as similar to Earth—the dead retain the same social status as they had in life, and require food, money, tools, and weapons. The Kachin help their dead relatives by placing these objects in their graves. The Sakai of Malaysia believe that the journey to the otherworld involves crossing a thin bamboo bridge above a ravine. Good souls cross the bridge without difficulty, but evil souls fall off into a cauldron of boiling water, where they remain until they are purified.

ANDREW CAMPBELL

Bibliography

Cotterell, Arthur. *Oxford Dictionary of World Mythology.* New York: Oxford University Press, 1986.

Knappert, Jan. *Mythology and Folklore in South-East Asia.* New York: Oxford University Press, 1999.

Scarre, Christopher, and Brian M. Fagan. *Ancient Civilizations.* New York: Longman, 1997.

Storm, Rachel. *Asian Mythology: Myths and Legends of China, Japan, Thailand, Malaysia and Indonesia.* London: Lorenz Books, 2000.

SEE ALSO: Ancestor Worship; Central Asia and the Steppes; China; Creation Myths; Death and the Afterlife; Flood Myths; India.

SPHINX

Crouching in front of the pyramids in Giza, Egypt, is one of the most mysterious statues ever built: the Great Sphinx, a hybrid creature with a lion's body and a human head. No one is sure of the purpose, if any, for which it was intended.

Who built the Sphinx? Why? When? This last question is perhaps the thorniest. The consensus among Egyptologists is that the face of the Sphinx is the image of Fourth Dynasty pharaoh Khafre (reigned c. 2540–2514 BCE), and was built by him to guard his eternal resting place. Some historians, however, believe that the Sphinx was built about 2650 BCE, shortly before the pyramids, and underwent substantial reworking at a later time. Still others have made the radical proposition that the massive statue is much older, predating the pyramids by thousands of years.

The statue in context

The three huge Fourth Dynasty (c. 2575–c. 2450 BCE) pyramids of Khufu, his son Khafre, and grandson Menkaure dominate the Giza Plateau near Cairo. Khafre's pyramid is the middle one of the three. It is the same size as the Great Pyramid of Khufu but appears larger because it is built on ground 33 feet (10 m) higher. From each pyramid a causeway led down to a valley temple alongside a canal from the Nile River. Khafre's body would have been received here and taken up the causeway to a mortuary temple and inside the pyramid to its burial chamber.

The causeway veers slightly southwest. Just off to its northern side sits the Great Sphinx. It faces east, toward the rising sun. It is 238 feet (72.5 m) long, around 66 feet (20 m) to the top of its head, and 40.6 feet (12.4 m) to the top of its back. A temple was built in front of the Sphinx, but never completed. This temple was very similar to the valley temple of Khafre exactly opposite it on the other side of the causeway, creating a striking symmetry.

Below: The Sphinx at Giza was hewn from the living rock of a limestone outcrop in the desert. Masonry was added as detail.

The Sphinx has the body of a lion and the head of a human. The head originally bore the traditional signs of a king or a god—a beard and a cobra. On the head is a *nemes*, a headdress of a type worn only by kings of ancient Egypt. The Sphinx has some traces of red paint, so at some time it was painted.

Today the Sphinx sits as a mute witness to the ravages of time. Many of its poor-quality limestone surface layers have been eroded by windblown sand from the surrounding desert. Some people have speculated that the damage was

Above: This line of crouching sphinxes stands at Luxor, near the ancient Egyptian city of Thebes. A Muslim minaret stands in the background.

caused by floodwater. If so, the statue is much older than generally thought, but this theory is controversial and not supported by most scholars. There is considerable damage to the face and ears. The royal cobra and beard are absent: fragments of them are in the British Museum in London, England, and the Cairo Museum, Egypt. Over the centuries there have been many attempts to restore the Sphinx. Some

The Riddle of the Sphinx

According to Greek legend, the Sphinx was the female offspring either of the monsters Typhon and Echidna or of the two-headed hound Orthus and the fire-breathing hybrid creature, the Chimaera. The Sphinx was sent by the goddess Hera to terrorize Thebes as a punishment for the Theban king Laius. Thebes was the principal urban center of Boeotia, one of the major ancient Greek city-states, and lay northwest of Athens. The monster installed herself on a high rock outside the gates of the city and devoured every passing traveler who failed to solve her riddle: "What has four legs in the morning, two legs in the afternoon, and three legs in the evening?"

The Thebans were desperate until the arrival of Greek hero Oedipus. He solved the riddle in a single word: "Man." He correctly deduced that humans crawl on all fours in infancy, walk upright as adults, and use walking sticks when they are old. On receiving this correct answer the Sphinx hurled herself to her death

on the rocks below. Oedipus was acclaimed as a savior. He was offered the throne of Thebes and the hand in marriage of the recently widowed queen, who turned out to be his own mother, Jocasta. The late king, Laius, had been murdered by Oedipus during a dispute about right-of-way as they passed each other on the road. Oedipus had no idea that the man he slew in this incident was a king, let alone his own father—uniquely among Greek tragic heroes, Oedipus had no tragic flaw: he was merely ill-fated.

The oldest surviving sources for the story of Oedipus and the Theban Sphinx are Homer (c. ninth–eighth century BCE) and Hesiod (fl. 800 BCE). The legend was later embellished by numerous other Greek authors, most notably the playwright Sophocles (c. 496–406 BCE). It is interesting to note that the Sphinx was regarded as a protector by Egyptians but as a monster by Greeks—her enigmatic facial expression fascinated the former, but seemed threatening to the latter.

Although many early Egyptologists thought that the Great Sphinx was connected with the pyramid of Khufu, modern scholars associate it more with the pyramid complex of his son, Khafre. Mark Lehner, a modern Egyptologist who has spent years studying the Great Sphinx, feels that it is in line with west Asian tradition to see the lion as both a symbol of the sun and of royalty. Using computer graphics, Lehner found a strong correlation between the face of the statue and images of Khafre. He theorizes that this fusion of king and sun god "symbolized power and might controled by the intelligence of the pharaoh, guarantor of cosmic order, or maat."

Sphinx as symbol

From the Middle Kingdom (c. 1938–c. 1630 BCE), pharaohs were commonly depicted as sphinxes. A sphinx in the Cairo Museum shows Amenemhet III (ruled 1842–1797 BCE) with a lion's mane and ears instead of the more usual nemes headdress. Another sphinx in Cairo shows the female pharaoh Hatshepsut (c. 1503–1482 BCE), also with the mane of a lion. A magnificent red granite sphinx of Hatshepsut in New York's Metropolitan Museum of Art has the nemes and beard; the cobra is broken away. There are also small blue faience examples of kings as sphinxes. The second largest sphinx is at Memphis, near Cairo. Its date is uncertain, but it is thought to be from the New Kingdom.

Royal jewelry often had a sphinx as a motif. A pendant of Queen Mereret, a wife of Senwosret III (ruled c. 1918–1875 BCE), shows the sphinx as falcon-headed. A carnelian bracelet piece shows Queen Tiy (fl. 1400 BCE), wife of Amenhotep III (1417–1379 BCE), as a winged female sphinx. Akhenaton (ruled c. 1379–1362 BCE) also had himself shown as a sphinx. Images of a sphinx appear on two kinds of objects from the tomb of Tutankhamen: wooden shields, and the end of a painted box on which a standing sphinx tramples Egypt's enemies.

ELIZABETH LONGLEY

Bibliography

Lehner, Mark. *The Complete Pyramids*. New York: Thames and Hudson, 1997.

Redford, Donald B. *The Ancient Gods Speak: A Guide to Egyptian Religion*. New York: Oxford University Press, Inc., 2002.

SEE ALSO: Animal-Headed Figures; Egypt; Oedipus.

were counterproductive, leading to further deterioration. Erosion caused by heavy rainwater continues to cause most damage to the surface of the Sphinx.

Was the Sphinx a god?

No one knows the purpose of the Great Sphinx. It does not carry the name of a god or a pharaoh. Its temple was unfinished and not dedicated to a specific deity. There is no evidence that it was associated with any god until the New Kingdom (c. 1540–c. 1075 BCE). More than 1,000 years after Khafre's pyramid was built, Amenhotep II (ruled c. 1450–1425 BCE) had a brick temple erected near the Sphinx and dedicated to the god Horemakhet, "Horus in the horizon." This renewed interest in the Great Sphinx was taken even further by his son, Thutmose IV (ruled 1425–1417 BCE). The 19th Dynasty pharaoh Seti I (ruled c. 1318–1304 BCE) added to the temple of Horemakhet. From the time of the New Kingdom, it was a place of pilgrimage. High and low Egyptians alike left stone tablets commemorating their visits. Pharaoh Tutankhamen (ruled c. 1361–1352 BCE) had a rest house at the site.

STARS

Humans have always been fascinated by stars. For thousands of years many peoples around the world relied on the position of certain stars in the night sky for their own survival. For instance, sailors used the stars to help them navigate the seas, and farmers relied on the annual movement of stars to judge the right time to plant or harvest crops. The objects in the sky were also mysterious and unreachable, however. For both these reasons, stars were integral to the belief systems of most early civilizations.

Scholars believe that nearly all ancient cultures thought that star clusters formed outlines of mythological characters or objects, and in many cases that individual stars represented gods or goddesses. In the Western world modern astronomy has inherited the star groupings—constellations—that were recognized by the ancient Greeks and Romans. The Greeks and Romans inherited their cosmology from the Egyptians, Mesopotamians, Canaanites, and other early Mediterranean cultures. Star groupings from other ancient cultures not necessarily known by the Greeks or Romans are generally referred to by modern astronomers as decans or asterisms. The ancient Egyptians, for example, saw lions, men, ox legs, and other beasts in the stars; these groupings rose once every ten days in Egypt and are all known today as decans.

Most of the names given to the constellations seen in the northern hemisphere were coined by the Romans.

Right: Movement of the stars during the night is captured in this long-exposure photograph.

Ursa Major and the Big Dipper

Some star clusters are not official constellations. An example is the star grouping that North Americans call the Big Dipper. In parts of Africa it is known as the Drinking Gourd, an object similar to a dipper. To modern astronomers, it is part of the constellation Ursa Major, which is Latin for "Great Bear," a title that originally came from the Greek myth of Callisto. Callisto was a nymph who was loved by Jupiter (Zeus) and bore him a son. She was changed into a bear by either Diana (Artemis) or Juno (Hera) and killed by her son, who did not realize that the bear was his mother. She was then transformed into the constellation.

Few other cultures, however, have seen the outline of a bear in Ursa Major or a dipper in the Big Dipper. In Great Britain the Big Dipper is seen as a plow. In other parts of Europe, it is known as the Wagon or Wain. The ancient Egyptians pictured it as the leg of a bull or ox. Nevertheless, the Big Dipper is important for navigation in all cultures of the northern hemisphere because it always points to Polaris, the north star. The handle of the Big Dipper, or tail of the Great Bear, points north in winter, east in spring, south in summer, and west in fall.

Left: Impressions of ancient Greek astrological figures, including a centaur and hydra, appear in this 16th-century fresco, which is painted on the dome of the old library at Salamanca University in Spain.

However, astronomers named most constellations seen in the southern hemisphere a couple of centuries ago, and these are not named for mythological characters.

In the ancient Greek and Roman worlds it was not uncommon for a single constellation to be connected with several myths. For example, the constellation Virgo was identified most often with Dike (goddess of justice), but was also known as Tyche (goddess of fate), Eos (goddess of dawn), Astraeia (daughter of Astraeus, father of the stars), and Erigone (daughter of Icarius—not to be confused with Icarus, son of Daedalus). A Roman writer named Hyginus, who lived during the first century BCE, claimed that Virgo represented Erigone. According to Hyginus, Dionysus, god of wine, taught Icarius how to cultivate grapevines and make wine. Icarius offered some of the wine he had made to his neighbors. The men drank the wine until they grew

drunk and passed out. Because no one had ever had wine or been intoxicated before, the families of the unconscious men thought that the men were dead. In anger, the others killed Icarius and left his body beneath a tree. Maera, Icarius's dog, led Erigone to the body. She was so overcome with grief at the death of her father that she hanged herself from the tree. The dog then pined away until it also died. The gods were so moved by the deaths of Icarius, Erigone, and Maera that they transformed each of them into a constellation. From then on, Virgo was sometimes known as Erigone, Boötes as Icarius, and Canis Major as Maera.

Naming planets

Myths that relate to stars are usually of one of two types: those that explain how the constellations came into existence, or those that talk about single stars or planets. Many ancient cultures mistook planets for stars. Primitive astronomy recognized seven celestial bodies: the sun, the moon, Mercury, Venus, Jupiter, Mars, and Saturn. Without visual aids, such as telescopes, the planets appear as very

Some Constellations Named for Greek Myths

Although the planets in our solar system and many constellations have names from Roman myths, some retain their older, Greek names. Most of these are either gods, heroes, or tragic characters from Greek myths or incidents referencing the myths. Below is a list of some Greek characters and myths, followed by constellations named for them.

Perseus
Perseus, Pegasus, Cassiopeia, and Andromeda

Voyage of the Argo
Puppis, Carina, and Vela (collectively Argo Navis)

Pleiades and Orion
Orion, Pleiades, Scorpio, and Taurus

Callisto
Ursa Major

Phrixus and Helle
Aries (also called the Ram)

Heracles
Hercules

Castor and Pollux
Gemini

Ariadne
Corona Borealis

Below: The planet Venus (at lower center) and the Pleiades are shown here over silhouetted trees in early morning. Venus has long been known as the morning star and evening star because it is never visible for more than three hours before sunrise or three hours after sunset.

bright stars. They are, however, easily distinguished from the other stars because they do not appear in the same place every night, and they are not part of a group. Because of their movement in the sky, these objects were called *planetes* by the ancient Greeks—their word for "wanderers."

The names for the planets in our solar system were chosen because of some quality that reminded the ancient Roman skywatchers of their divine namesakes. For example, since Mercury is the closest planet to the sun, its orbit is quickest. Although ancient astronomers did not know that Earth and the other planets orbited the sun, they could see that Mercury moved through the night sky quicker than other objects. They named the planet for the messenger of the Olympian gods, Mercury, who traveled quickly because of the wings on his sandals. By contrast, Saturn has a very long orbit and moves slowly across the sky. It was named for the Titan Saturn, sometimes known as the god of time. As the largest object in the night sky, except for the moon, it was natural that the planet Jupiter should be identified with the king of the gods, Jupiter.

(1855–1916) predicted the planet's existence before he died, but another American astronomer, Clyde W. Tombaugh (1906–1997), found the distant planet. Pluto was so hard to find it was named for the Roman god of the underworld, because he could make himself invisible. Pluto is our solar system's smallest planet. At the planet's equator its diameter is calculated to be 1,423 miles (2,290 km). In 2004, astronomers claimed to have discovered a 10th planet, which they named for the Inuit goddess Sedna. Sedna, however, is even smaller than Pluto, and most astronomers believe that it is not large enough to be truly called a planet.

Names from other ancient cultures

Prior to the Greeks and Romans, other great Mediterranean cultures also identified the planets with gods. The Mesopotamians saw the planet Venus as their goddess of love and fertility, Inanna (Ishtar) or Astarte (this may have been a source for the Romans' choosing their goddess of love as the name of the planet). The planet Venus appears in either the morning or evening sky and has been known as the morning star or evening star, respectively. The morning star was often given the name of a male god, while the evening star was usually thought of as a female deity. Inanna was the personification of the evening star. Her symbol was an eight-pointed star. The ancient Canaanites named the morning star Ashtar, favorite son of the great goddess Asherah.

The ancient Egyptians relied on the stars to provide an annual flood warning. They learned that when Orion disappeared and Sirius appeared the Nile River would soon rise and flood its basin. The Nile basin is the most fertile region of Egypt, and being able to predict the flood season was essential to maintaining a good harvest. Nonetheless, scholars do not know the Egyptian names of many constellations and stars. The star called Sirius, however, is one exception. It is thought that for centuries the Egyptians called the star Sepdet—but changed it to Sothis in later years. They identified it with the goddess Isis. Isis was the widow of Osiris, who was linked to the constellation Orion, which the Egyptians called Sahu.

Although it appears that the ancient Egyptians did not name Ursa Major (see box, page 1334), they did depict it. They imagined the constellation as the leg of an ox thrown into the heavens by the god Seth. In paintings the

Mars has a reddish appearance and was identified with the blood-soaked god of war. Venus is the brightest star, so it was named after the Roman goddess of beauty.

Modern sightings, ancient names

In modern times, as astronomers discovered that there are more planets in our solar system than the five—plus Earth—named by the Romans, the convention of using the names of Roman gods continued. Uranus, the sky and father of Saturn and the other Titans, was used for the name of the seventh planet in the solar system. It was first spotted by William Herschel in 1781. The eighth planet is Neptune, named after the god of the sea. A theory about its existence was announced in 1820, but it was not observed and named until 1846. Pluto, the ninth planet, was discovered in 1930. American astronomer Percival Lowell

leg was sometimes showed tethered to a pole. The tether showed that the group of stars rotated around the celestial north pole.

Some Japanese names for stars

In Japan most modern names for constellations come from Western sources. Some constellations and star clusters that have the names of mythological characters, such as Andromeda, are written in katakana—the Japanese script used for scientific terms and foreign words—and sound similar to their English counterparts. Most of the Western star groupings identified as objects have been renamed with somewhat similar objects common to traditional Japanese culture. For example, in the West the constellation Lyra, of which Vega is the brightest star, refers to a lyre, an ancient Greek stringed instrument similar to a harp. Orpheus was able to produce hypnotically beautiful music when he played the lyre. In Japan the constellation Lyra is known as Koto. A koto is an ancient Japanese stringed musical instrument that is actually more like a zither than a lyre.

Other modern names merely translate the Latin or Greek word. For example, in Greek mythology Aquila was the eagle that carried Zeus's thunderbolts. In Japan the constellation Aquila is called Washi, which means "eagle." The history behind the Japanese names for Ursa Major and Ursa Minor is more complicated. Ursa Major is called Ooguma, and Ursa Minor is called Koguma. The

Chinese Constellations

In China the stars and planets were traditionally represented as emperors, empresses, or other court figures. Paintings from the 12th century CE show the planets as richly dressed figures with elaborate headgear. Mars is depicted as a red-faced man, perhaps a courtier. Jupiter is represented as a large portly figure, maybe a court servant, holding a tray with four peaches. The peaches stand for the moons that revolve around the giant planet.

Most of the traditional Chinese star groupings are different from those used in the West. For example, the constellation Orion is broken up into several smaller clusters. There are other Chinese names for constellations or star clusters that are recognized in the West. The three stars that form Orion's belt, for instance, are called the Three Generals. Yu Ya (the Chariot) is the seven bright stars of the Great Bear, Qu is the bear's tail, and San Tai are the feet. Tai Jiao, meaning "the great horn," is the star Arcturus. Fang Nu (the Spinning Damsel) includes Vega and some neighboring stars in the constellation Lyra. Tian He (Celestial River), or Yin He (Silver River), is the name for our Milky Way. The stars above the North Pole, which never drop below the horizon, are collectively known as either Ce Kong or Ce Wei Yuan.

Below: This 1911 reproduction of an original 19th-century image depicts five Chinese spirits who represent the planets Mercury, Mars, Venus, Jupiter, and Saturn.

Above: The Origin of the Milky Way *by Tintoretto (c. 1518–1594). In this painting, Roman goddess Juno suckles the infant Hercules. Milk that flowed from her breasts supposedly formed the Milky Way.*

astronomical names for the constellations appear to come from Greek mythology, as Ooguma and Koguma mean Big Bear and Little, or Child, Bear respectively. However, the word *kuma* (or *guma*), which forms the suffix of *Ooguma* and *Koguma*, can mean either "bear," "corner," or "nook." Before Western influence changed the meanings of Japanese-known star clusters, Ooguma and Koguma meant "Big Corner" and "Little Corner."

The southernmost star of the Big Dipper portion of Ursa Major is called Alkaid in the West and Hagunsei in Japanese. *Hagunsei* literally means "the military breaking star," but it can also mean "most corner star." Both meanings come from ancient China's influence on Japan. In Chinese fortune-telling, north is believed to be a very unlucky direction. Northwest is even worse. Hunters and soldiers traditionally did not point guns or weapons in the direction of Hagunsei.

Japanese explanation for Orion

Star groupings that would appear in the east at sunset and set with the dawning sun were called *yowatashi boshi*, Japanese for "passing the night stars." In Japan, as in almost every other culture in the northern hemisphere, Orion is one of the most recognizable *yowatashi boshi* in the night sky. In ancient Egypt, Greece, and Rome, the constellation appeared to resemble the outline of a man with broad shoulders and a narrow waist. In Japan the constellation is called Tsuzumi Boshi. The *tsuzumi* is a Japanese drum played at both ends and used in the theater and in music performed at the imperial court. The musical instrument is shaped almost like an hourglass, with strings securing the drum faces to each other. It was the outline of the drum that the ancient Japanese saw in Orion. The stars that form Orion's torso and hips for the West are the two ends of the drum for the Japanese. The three belt stars, or *mitsu boshi*, represent the cord used to tie the strings in the middle of the instrument. In some parts of Japan the constellation is seen differently. For example, some see the shape of a *sode boshi*, or kimono sleeve, in the star grouping. Kimono sleeves are long, rectangular, and hang almost to the ground. Some Japanese skywatchers saw in Orion a woman with the long sleeve of her kimono hanging down from an outstretched arm.

The sisters and the demons

The origin of the kimono sleeve image may have come from a myth that tells of the forming of the constellation Orion, or Tsuzumi Boshi. One day two sisters were walking down the road. The younger sister walked behind the elder one carrying a tub of water on a bamboo pole. They were stopped by demons called *oni*. The sisters turned and ran from the demons, but the oni chased after them. While running, the sisters saw a rope, hanging from the sky, magically appear in front of them. The sisters climbed up the rope to escape the demons. The elder sister went first and escaped unscathed. When she reached the top of the rope, she was transformed into the moon.

The younger sister, however, was not so lucky. The oni bit off her foot. Nevertheless she kept on climbing, and when she reached the heavens she was changed into the constellation Tsuzumi Boshi. For the ancient Japanese, the younger sister still followed the other (the moon) across the night sky. As for the younger sister's foot, its outline is supposed to be visible in the folds of the girl's kimono.

Other surviving constellation myths from ancient Japan describe how some brothers were also chased by oni and then turned into star groupings. In one myth, seven brothers became the Big Dipper; and in another, several brothers (the numbers vary) became the tail, or stinger, stars of the constellation Scorpio.

The Pawnee and the Swimming Ducks

For Native Americans the Pawnee, who lived in Kansas and Nebraska, the night sky was used as a kind of calendar, and the stars foretold the changing of the seasons. In February, for example, the Pawnee looked for the return of the "Swimming Ducks" in the dawn sky. These stars signaled the coming of spring: the stars' presence low in the south-southeast corner of the sky reminded the skywatchers of waterfowl breaking through the winter ice. However, most importantly for the Pawnee, who were nomadic hunters, the appearance of the Swimming Ducks was a sign that large game, particularly bison, would

Below: An English agricultural calendar from the 14th century. The figures in the top row are performing tasks that need to be done at particular times of the year. Each of these times is associated with a different sign of the zodiac, depicted in the bottom row.

Left: Orion is one of the most recognizable constellations in the northern sky.

star constellation that they thought of as representing six women: in their version the women lived at the end of the world beyond the horizon. Their neighbors, the Yokuts, described the stars as five wives and their one husband.

In the southern hemisphere a similar constellation exists, known as the Southern Pleiades. In Australia the Aborigines saw the stars of this group as wives waiting for their husbands. The husbands would never come home. As the myth goes, the husbands broke one of the laws set down by the sun and were sucked into the sky.

Agni and Krttika

In the *Mahabharata*, an epic poem of ancient Hindu mythology, the Pleiades were seven women called the Krttika. Originally the women were happily married to the seven stars of the Big Dipper. These stars were called the Rishi, meaning "wise men." Their happy relationships ended when Agni, god of fire, caught sight of the beautiful Krttika. He proposed to each of the women, but all of them turned him down. Hurt by the rejection, Agni hid in the forest. There he was seen by the goddess Svaha, who could take the form of a star. Svaha fell in love with Agni, but just as the Krttika had rejected Agni, Agni rejected Svaha.

Not willing to give up, Svaha disguised herself as one of the Krttika and seduced Agni. Pleased with her success, she went on to disguise herself as each of the other six Krttika. However, the seventh time she tried to make love to Agni, the fire god realized it was a trick, because the seventh Krttika was well known to be devoted to her husband.

The myth also tells that Svaha used a unique form of contraception. She collected Agni's semen in a cave and so did not get pregnant, despite having made love to him six times. The cave gave birth to a boy called Skanda. Rumors spread that the six Krttika were the child's mothers, and the Rishi divorced their wives. The six Krttika, wrongly accused, were then sent to another part of the night sky.

LYN GREEN

be returning to the Great Plains. Some historians believe that the Swimming Ducks, like the Japanese brothers, may have been the stars in the tail of the constellation Scorpio.

The Pleiades

The Pleiades constellation was named by many ancient cultures in the northern hemisphere. It looks like a tiny dipper of six moderately bright stars. In ancient Japanese cosmology, for instance, the Pleiades is called Subaru. Women are a constant theme in stories about the Pleiades. According to the legends of the Ainu people of northern Japan, the stars were six lazy girls. Across the Pacific Ocean in California, the Yurok Native Americans also saw a six-

Bibliography
Ridpath, Ian. *Smithsonian Handbooks: Stars and Planets.* New York: Dorling Kindersley, 2002.
Sasaki, Chris. *The Constellations: Stars and Stories.* New York: Sterling Publishing, 2001.

SEE ALSO: Ariadne; Calendars; Callisto; Castor and Pollux; China; Egypt; Eos; Festivals; Heracles; Jupiter; Mars; Mercury; Moon; Orion; Perseus; Pleiades; Saturn; Sky; Sun; Uranus; Venus.

SUN

Ancient peoples all over the world worshiped the sun, often as one of the most important deities in their pantheon. While the sun was regarded as male in some cultures and female in others, a constant theme was the sun's importance to life on Earth. Some myths focused on the journey of the sun across the sky; others on conflicts between the sun and other beings. Behind these stories, however, lay the threat of what would happen if the sun ceased to shine.

One of the best known sun-worshiping cultures was that of ancient Egypt. The original Egyptian sun god was Re, who was usually depicted as a falcon- or hawk-headed man with a red disk on his head, representing the sun. The ancient Egyptians explained the daily passage of the sun across the sky in terms of a journey Re undertook in a boat. At sunset, they believed that Re and his boat passed into the underworld, where the god battled with the demonic serpent Apophis. Consequently, even though Egyptians could not see the sun god after nightfall, they knew he was engaged in a vitally important struggle. If he lost the fight, eternal darkness would cover the earth. In the underworld part of his journey, Re took on the name of Atum, the creator of the universe. In the morning, when the sun rose again, Re was known as Khepra and was depicted with the head of a scarab, or dung beetle. Egyptian priests likened the flaming ball of the morning sun to a ball of dung, pushed along by the beetle. Like Re as Atum, Re as Khepra was regarded as a god of

Right: The sun is the most important and most obvious object in the sky, and its light and warmth make life on Earth possible. It is not surprising that it was worshiped in many ancient cultures.

creation. The god's dung beetle aspect was appropriate in this creative sense, too: female dung beetles lay their eggs in dung balls.

Re was identified with a number of other important gods in ancient Egypt. One such deity was the sun god Horakhty, or "Horus of the two horizons." Horus was a popular name for Egyptian deities—there were around 20 Horuses in the pantheon—while the "two horizons" refer to where the sun rises and sets. Over time, this sun god merged with Re to become Re-horakhty.

Another god who was identified with Re was Amun, the ram-headed god of Thebes in Upper Egypt. In the second millennium BCE, Amun became the preeminent deity of the early Egyptian Empire. His followers utilized the power and prestige of Re to give Amun greater importance, naming him Amun-Re. Depictions of the god began to include a sun disk on his head to show that he, too, had become a solar god. However, evidence from tomb paintings and Books of the Dead—placed in tombs to help guide the dead in the afterlife—suggests that many Egyptians continued to believe in Re as the most important manifestation of the sun.

After around 1075 BCE, the same religious syncretism, or merging, that had seen Re identified with Horakhty and Amun led the god to be harmonized with Osiris, the god of death and resurrection. Osiris slowly took over Re's most important responsibilities, eventually replacing the sun god as the most important figure in the Egyptian pantheon.

Other west Asian sun myths

In contrast to the ancient Egyptians, the Mesopotamians never put the sun at the top of their pantheon. Perhaps this was because Mesopotamia, the land between the Tigris and Euphrates rivers where Iraq now lies, was a cooler region than Egypt, with more variable weather. The Sumerians, who dominated southern Mesopotamia from around 3000 to approximately 1900 BCE, called their sun god Utu. There are no specific Sumerian myths about Utu, but the god appears in stories about other deities. For example, in the story of Inanna, the love goddess who sends her husband Dumuzi to the underworld as a punishment, Utu offers the unfortunate Dumuzi his help.

The Babylonians dominated Mesopotamia between around 1900 and 539 BCE. Their equivalent of the sun god Utu was Shamash, an all-seeing god who was linked to justice. The Babylonians

Left: An Egyptian pillar, c. 1100–650 BCE, is decorated with an image of Re-horakhty (left) and an attendant.

Worshiping the Sun-Disk

The pharaoh Amenhotep IV (ruled 1379–1362 BCE) is perhaps the most famous sun worshiper of all. He attempted to replace all the old gods with a little-known deity called Aten (or Aton). The word *aten* means "sun-disk" and referred to the physical sun in the sky. The pharaoh gave Aten a personality and a new image. Amenhotep himself took the name *Akhenaton*, meaning "devotee of Aten." He built a new city between Thebes and Memphis known as Akhetaton, meaning "the horizon of Aten." Hymns declared Aten to be the pharaoh's father, as well as the caretaker and lifegiver of everything on earth. The deity was depicted as a disk or ball in the sky, with hands reaching down to touch the pharaoh and his family and to receive offerings.

However, despite all Amenhotep's efforts, Aten never became widely popular, and images of the god were even defaced after the pharaoh's death. People resented Amenhotep's attempts to overthrow the powerful priests of the old gods and wipe away thousands of years of religious tradition. Inevitably, the pharaoh's behavior especially angered the priests themselves. Ordinary Egyptians may have cared little about the priests' power, but the greatest failing of the sun-disk religion was that it had no myths to attract the affection of worshipers. Aten did not appear in any myths or stories, and the new belief system never developed a vision of the afterlife to replace the worship of Osiris.

Right: A limestone carving of Egyptian pharaoh Amenhotep IV and his wife, Nefertiti (c. 1365–1347 BCE). Amenhotep attempted to make veneration of the sun-disk Aten central to ancient Egyptian religion.

believed that Shamash's piercing rays of light allowed him to spot all human misdeeds and gave him the means to see into the future. Shamash's journey across the sky was imagined differently than from that of Re. The Babylonian god came out of a gate in the enormous mountain of Mashu every morning. Riding in a chariot, he ascended the mountain until he was at the top of the sky, then crossed the sky until he came to another mountain, where he passed out of view and through another gate. At nighttime, Shamash traveled deep beneath the earth before returning to Mount Mashu.

Like the Sumerians and the Babylonians, the people of Ugarit did not place their sun deity at the head of their pantheon. Ugarit, which flourished between approximately 1450 and 1200 BCE, was an important city in an area of modern Syria. Its sun deity, Shapash, was female. She was the messenger of El, the lord of heaven, and in her journeys through the heavens during the day and the underworld at night was aware of everything that went on in both realms. In one myth, the goddess Anat sent Shapash to find the body of her brother, the storm god Baal, who had died in the underworld. Shapash found the body and, at the end of the story, was asked to rule over the spirits of the dead.

The Hittites, who flourished in Turkey between approximately 1850 and 1170 BCE, also worshiped a sun goddess. Most references to the deity describe her simply as the sun goddess of Arinna—the name of the town in which she was chiefly worshiped—but she may also have been known as Eshtan or Ishtan.

The Greeks and the sun

The ancient Greeks also worshiped the sun as a god, but they placed little emphasis on the provision of light and the vanquishing of darkness. They were more concerned with the particular qualities of their solar deity. Each day the Greeks' sun god, Helios, rode a chariot drawn by fiery

Above: The remains of a temple dedicated to the Hittite sun goddess of Arinna were found on the site of the Hittite capital city, Hattushash.

horses across the sky and, like the Babylonian Shamash and the Ugarit Shapash, was believed to see and hear everything on his travels. Helios's all-seeing nature played a part in a number of myths. In one, he told the fertility goddess Demeter that her daughter Persephone had been kidnapped by Hades, the lord of the underworld. In another, the sun god told Hephaestus, blacksmith of the gods, how he had observed his wife, the love goddess Aphrodite, committing adultery with Ares, god of war.

The journey of the sun god's chariot across the sky is central to another myth, which involved Helios's son Phaethon. When Helios promised to give Phaethon whatever his heart desired, the boy declared that he wanted to ride Helios's chariot across the sky. Helios knew that his son, a mere demigod, could not possibly control the immortal horses and the chariot, but he had given his word and had to agree to the boy's request. The father's

fears were well founded: when the unsteady Phaethon swung the chariot too close to the earth and set it on fire, Zeus was forced to strike him down with a thunderbolt. The boy's body fell into the Eridanus River, alongside which his sisters wept for him until the gods turned them into trees.

Although Apollo was originally worshiped as the god of music, prophecy, healing, and the protection of flocks and herds, the ancient Greeks began to link him with the sun, too. The poet Homer (c. ninth–eighth century BCE) called the god Phoebus Apollo, meaning "shining Apollo," and by the fifth century BCE the deity was regarded as a sun god and was sometimes identified with Helios. Like Helios and sun deities in a variety of other cultures, Apollo was paired with a deity representing the moon. In Apollo's case, this role was taken by his twin sister, Artemis. However, despite his role as a god of the sun, Apollo seems to have devoted more attention to other tasks and responsibilities, as well as to his amorous pursuit of women and nymphs.

Amaterasu, the Japanese sun goddess

Amaterasu was the supreme deity of the Shinto religion of Japan and was queen of all the Kami, the forces of nature. According to Shinto tradition, the sun goddess showed humans how to make food, clothing, and dwellings. Amaterasu's parents were the creator god and goddess Izanagi and Izanami. Her siblings were the moon god Tsuki-yomi and the storm god Susanowo. Susanowo and Amaterasu frequently argued and could not tolerate each other's presence for long—much like storm and sunshine can rarely share the same sky. According to the myth, one day Susanowo made so much noise visiting his sister that his thunder shook the mountains and sent all living beings into hiding. Even Amaterasu became frightened by the storm and armed herself with a bow and arrows.

When she saw her brother, she demanded proof that he meant her no harm. Susanowo responded by suggesting that he and his sister create children who would rule the world wisely. Amaterasu agreed. Taking her brother's sword, she broke it into three pieces. After chewing the pieces for many days and nights, she spat out three goddesses, who were more beautiful than anyone else except for their mother. Susanowo then asked his sister for the five jewels she was wearing, and after cracking them between his teeth, spat out five gods who were more powerful than anyone else, except for their father. Susanowo then began to boast that he was the most powerful of all the gods. Amaterasu replied by reminding him that his gods had been created from her jewels. Her response enraged Susanowo. He released the wind and rain he held beneath his arms, destroying his sister's rice fields and irrigation ditches and filling her temple with mud.

In protest at her brother's behavior, Amaterasu withdrew into a cave, plunging the world into darkness. Without the light and warmth of the sun, all living things began to wither and die. The other gods tried to coax Amaterasu out, but she refused. Ama no Uzume, the goddess of joy, happiness, and the dawn, came to the rescue. Wearing nothing but leaves and flowers, she began to dance on an upturned tub. Attracted by the noise, Amaterasu peered out of the cave to see what all the commotion was about. Behind Ama no Uzume was hidden a great octagonal mirror. When Amaterasu appeared, Ama no Uzume moved aside to allow two gods to roll the mirror in front of the

Below: A second-century-BCE Greek frieze of the sun god Helios. The sculpture depicts rays of light emerging from Helios's head, while the god's horses, who pull his chariot, dominate the foreground.

Above: The Japanese sun goddess Amaterasu emerges from the cave, enticed out by the noises made by Ama no Uzume. This screen painting is by Japanese artist Utagawa Kunisada (1786–1864).

cave. Amaterasu, who had never seen her own beauty before, was delighted. She returned to take her place in the world, allowing life to flourish once more.

Native American sun myths

Like Japanese beliefs, in many Native American myths the sun was female, and like ancient Greek beliefs, many Native American myths depicted the sun and moon as siblings. The Maidu of California believed that the sun and the moon, her brother, lived together in a house below the eastern horizon. They were so fond of their home that they would not leave it. The other gods realized that there would never be enough light unless the sun and moon were in the sky, so they made a plan to force the pair out by infesting their house with fleas. It worked. Once outside, the two decided to cross the sky. However, they did not want to travel together. The moon suggested that his sister travel at night and he would cross the heavens by day. However, because the sun was so beautiful, all the stars fell in love with her and tried to prevent her from leaving the

sky. The siblings rearranged their schedules: the moon traveled by night and the sun by day.

The Inuit of Canada also pictured the sun as a beautiful female. Her brother, the moon, was far less attractive both physically and in terms of personality. The moon lusted after his sister but knew that she would never commit incest. To trick the sun, the moon covered his face with ashes and crept into her bed at night. His ruse succeeded— in the morning the sun was horrified to discover what she had done. She swore that her brother would never touch her again, but he merely laughed. He told her that he was stronger than she and would do as he pleased. The sun responded by grabbing a torch and fleeing into the sky. Her brother took another torch and chased after her, but he could never catch up. Each night he dropped a little farther behind. In this way the Inuit explained the sun's passage across the sky followed by the moon, and the fact that the moon appears to be moving farther away from the sun each night.

Aztec and Inca sun gods

Many ancient peoples in Mexico and Central and South America regarded the sun as a very important deity. Two famous sun gods were Huitzilopochtli, worshiped by the

Aztecs of Mexico, and Inti, worshiped by the Incas of Peru. As well as being a sun deity, Huitzilopochtli was the god of war and human sacrifice. The Aztecs believed that human sacrifice was a vital part of worshiping the sun. According to the Aztec religion, the sun required human blood to quench its thirst. If this blood was not forthcoming, the sun would stand still in the sky and its rays would burn up the earth. Besides offering up their own people, the Aztecs made war on their neighbors to obtain additional sacrifices for Huitzilopochtli.

Inti, the Inca sun god, was conventionally depicted as a human figure with a gold disk for a face, out of which came flames and rays of light. Inti was another example of a sun god with a moon deity for a sibling. His sister, who was also his wife, was the moon goddess Mama-Kilya. She was also depicted as a human figure, but she had a silver disk for a face.

Below: The Ise-Jingu, the most sacred shrine to Amaterasu. Some events in the coronation of each Japanese emperor takes place at the shrine, since it is believed that the imperial family is descended from her.

Amaterasu, Ancestor of Emperors

In addition to her role as a sun goddess, Amaterasu was the ancestor of the imperial house of Japan. According to myth, she sent her grandson Ninigi to conquer and pacify the Japanese islands. To help him carry out this task, Amaterasu gave Ninigi a mirror, sword, and jewels—sacred objects that became symbols of the Japanese Empire. The first Japanese emperor, Jimmu Tenno of probably the seventh century BCE, was believed to be Ninigi's great-grandson. To this day, an important part of the emperor's coronation ceremony takes place at Amaterasu's main temple, which houses the sacred mirror, in the city of Ise on the island of Honshu. Amaterasu's emblem, the rising sun, appears on Japan's flag, and the goddess herself is celebrated every July 17. During this celebration, known as the Great Festival of the Sun Goddess, parades occur throughout the day. Another holiday in honor of the goddess is held on December 21, on the eve of the winter solstice. This festival commemorates the goddess's emergence from her cave, to warm the earth and allow life to flourish.

Above: This 19th-century Native American chief's ceremonial headdress represents the sun. During ceremonial dances the mask would reflect firelight, giving the impression of a glowing sun.

Inti was regarded as the ancestor of the Incas. The founder of the Inca Empire, Pachacuti Yupanqui Inca, was closely associated with the god: an annual ceremony involved relocating the ruler's body from his palace tomb to the temple of the sun god. Inca astrologers observed Inti's course from east to west across the sky in their efforts to predict the future. The Inca ruins at Machu Picchu, high in the Andes Mountains of Peru, provide one example of how the astrologers worked: the site contains large stone pillars that formed a shadow clock.

An African sun myth

The Ewe of western Africa believed the sun and moon were sisters who each gave birth to many stars. According to myth, one day the sun invited her sister to a large feast, consisting of all her children, whom she had killed for the moon to eat. The moon ate with relish and, when she had finished, invited her sister for a reciprocal meal. However, by the time the sun arrived at her sister's house, the moon had hidden her children in a huge pot. The sun had to go away hungry. After this occasion, the moon never dared to release her children while their aunt was around, although they traveled the sky with their mother at night.

LYN GREEN

Bibliography

Ferguson, Diana. *Tales of the Plumed Serpent: Aztec, Inca, and Mayan Myths.* New York: Sterling, 2000.

Howatson, M. C., and Ian Chilvers. *Concise Oxford Companion to Classical Literature.* New York: Oxford University Press, 1993.

McCall, Henrietta. *Mesopotamian Myths.* Austin, TX: University of Texas Press, 1991.

Redford, Donald B. *The Oxford Essential Guide to Egyptian Mythology.* New York: Oxford University Press, 2003.

SEE ALSO: Africa; Animal-Headed Figures; Apollo; Artemis; Aztecs; Cycles; Egypt; Helios; Inanna; Inca; Mesopotamia; Moon; Native Americans; Natural Forces; Osiris; Phaethon; Re; Sacrifice.

TANTALUS

Tantalus is famous for spending eternity reaching for tempting fruit that always moved away from his grasp at the last moment. This was his punishment for a series of crimes that offended the gods.

Tantalus was the son of Zeus and the Oceanid Pluto (not to be confused with the Roman god of the dead, who was also known as Pluto). Tantalus was a king, but different versions of the story disagree about where he ruled. Some say he lived at Sipylus and ruled the kingdom of Lydia (in modern Turkey); others say he was king of Phrygia or Paphlagonia (also in modern Turkey). Ancient Greek geographer Pausanias (143–176 CE) reported that Tantalus's tomb was on Mount Sipylus, and modern archaeologists have identified various sites that might correspond to it. However, the myth of Tantalus does not reveal enough to connect the mythical Tantalus to a historical person.

According to the myth, Tantalus married twice and had several children. His daughter Niobe insulted the gods by claiming that her own children were more beautiful and worthy of praise than them. To punish her, the gods Leto, Apollo, and Artemis killed the children, and Niobe was turned into a stone that stood on Mount Sipylus.

Tragedy continued down Tantalus's family line. His grandsons included Atreus and Thyestes, who feuded bitterly over the throne of Mycenae. This feud continued into the next generation when Aegisthus, son of Thyestes, murdered Agamemnon, son of Atreus (Agamemnon was the commander of the Greek army that besieged the city of Troy.)

Tantalus also upset the gods in various ways. As a son of Zeus, he was welcomed by the gods, who invited him to eat with them on Mount Olympus. At dinner, his table manners were terrible and offended the gods, and he could not resist stealing some of their food—nectar and ambrosia—and taking it to share with his human friends. He also gave away secrets that the gods had discussed over the meal.

Another of Tantalus's crimes was described by some writers as being more serious. He held a feast for the gods—some claim to apologize for his earlier behavior—but he also decided to test whether the gods were as all-knowing as people reputed them to be. He killed his own son, Pelops, then cooked him in a stew and served it up at

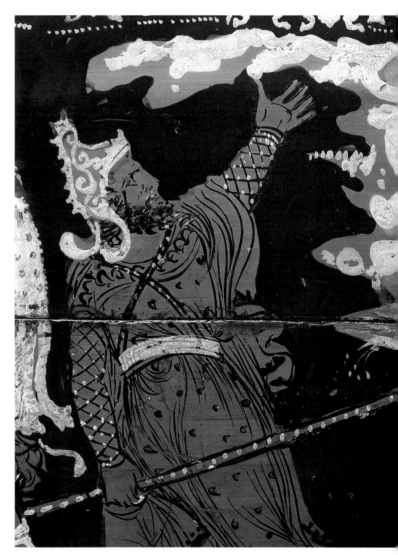

Right: The myth of Tantalus was a common source for ancient artists. King Tantalus is depicted reaching for fruit in this fourth-century-BCE vase painting.

In Tartarus, the part of the underworld where sinners were punished, Tantalus was forced to stand up to his chin in a pool of fresh water, but whenever he tried to lower his mouth to the water to drink, the water level dropped and he could not reach it. Hanging above the pool were tree branches laden with delicious ripe fruit; but when Tantalus tried to reach for some, the wind blew the branches aside so that he could never quite touch them. According to some versions, Zeus also balanced a massive boulder above Tantalus so that as well as suffering from eternal hunger and thirst, he was constantly nervous about the boulder crushing him.

Tantalus's fate served as an example to others, warning them not to upset the gods, and many ancient Greek and Roman writers retold his story. In the *Odyssey* by Homer (c. ninth–eighth century BCE), for example, the hero Odysseus recounts the sight of Tantalus suffering when he visited the land of the dead, and describes the "pear-trees and pomegranates, apple-trees with their glossy burden, sweet figs and luxuriant olives" that were tormenting Tantalus. Other writers who recorded the story of Tantalus include Apollodorus (third century BCE), Hyginus (first century BCE), Ovid (43 BCE–17 CE), and Plutarch (c. 46–120 CE).

Because it makes such a striking visual image, Tantalus's punishment has appeared countless times in art from ancient to modern times.

Tantalus today

Today the details of Tantalus's life are not well known, but his punishment in the underworld is famous and has become a part of modern language. His name came to form the common word *tantalize,* which means to tempt someone, usually with something they cannot have. A tantalus is also a kind of cabinet that shows its contents but locks so that a key is needed to access the items.

ANNA CLAYBOURNE

Bibliography
Homer, and Robert Fagles, trans. *The Odyssey*. New York: Penguin USA, 1999.
Ovid, and A. D. Melville, trans. *Metamorphoses*. New York: Oxford University Press, 1998.

SEE ALSO: Agamemnon; Demeter; Pelops; Zeus.

the feast to see if the gods would notice. The gods did indeed know what had happened, and most of them refused to eat the stew. However, Demeter, goddess of crops, was in mourning for her daughter Persephone, who had been stolen away to the underworld. She absent-mindedly ate Pelops's shoulder. The gods managed to bring the boy back to life, giving him an ivory shoulder to replace the one that had been eaten; but they never forgave Tantalus for his deceptive evil act.

The golden dog

Tantalus was also said to have stolen a golden dog belonging to Zeus—or to have persuaded a man named Pandareos to steal it for him. When challenged, Tantalus swore in the name of his father Zeus that he knew nothing about the dog. Zeus was so angry about the lie that he used a huge rock from Mount Sipylus to crush Tantalus to death. The king was carried off to the underworld, where an even worse fate awaited him.

Minoans and Mycenaeans in Crete

Theseus's liberation of Athens from paying tribute to Crete by killing the Minotaur is a mythical event. However, there is a historical parallel: the Mycenaeans, Greek-speaking people inhabiting the area we now know as Greece, overthrew the Minoan civilization on Crete in about 1400 BCE. Perhaps the historical event lies behind the story of Theseus's killing of the Minotaur.

Archaeologists who have examined ruins of the Minoan civilization on Crete, including ancient records of trade transactions between Cretans and other Mediterranean nations, speculate that there were a number of causes for the downfall of the Minoans. One popular explanation is that there was an enormous volcanic eruption on a nearby island around 1600 BCE that led to widespread devastation in the area. Tidal waves apparently traveled from the center of the eruption to northern Crete, where they demolished many palaces, including Knossos itself.

After the catastrophe some Minoan survivors migrated to mainland Greece, and those that stayed were later subjugated by invading Mycenaeans. Archaeologists and historians suggest that evidence of an invasion of Crete is indicated by the existence of two different languages on many ancient Cretan trade documents. They argue that Minoan scribes were recording transactions in a Minoan form and in another language that their new rulers, the Mycenaeans, could understand.

Right: Although most of the palace of Knossos was devastated around 1500 BCE, some parts still stand, including the northwest portico, pictured here.

made his way through the Labyrinth so that he would not get lost. Eventually Theseus confronted the Minotaur and, using a sword, club, or his hands, killed it. Then, retracing his steps using the thread, Theseus and the others made their way safely out of the Labyrinth. Theseus then set sail for Athens, taking Ariadne with him.

However, Theseus abandoned Ariadne on the first island they came to—some say it was the little island of Dia, but a more common myth claims it was Naxos. Before leaving Ariadne, Theseus gave to her the crown that he had received from Amphitrite. Dionysus, god of wine, saw the lonely princess and rescued her. According to one version of the myth, he put the crown into the sky, and it is now known as the constellation Corona, the Crown.

When Theseus had left Athens, he had told his father that he would change the sails of his ship from a dark color to white if his expedition was successful, but

Theseus forgot his promise. From his position on a cliff top, Aegeus saw Theseus's ship return but saw that its sails were dark. Believing that his son was dead, he threw himself into the sea. Legend has it that this is how the Aegean Sea received its name.

Following Aegeus's death, Theseus became king of Athens. He made the city strong and prosperous, and he became known for his wisdom and compassion. Various myths say that Theseus greatly improved the lives of the citizens. Developments were credited to him that were in fact instituted over several hundred years. Various legends claim that he united all of the small villages around Athens into a single political unit, over which he ruled. Theseus also supposedly instituted the Panathenaia, the all-Athens festival that Athenians celebrated each year in honor of Athena, goddess of war. In many legends about Theseus, he is not only revered as a great hero but also remembered as a great political leader.

Above: In this painting Venetian artist Vittore Carpaccio (c. 1460–1526) depicts an Amazon embassy meeting with an Athenian court to demand the return of their queen, whom Theseus had taken as his wife.

Other myths

According to one myth, Theseus accompanied Heracles on his ninth labor to retrieve the belt of Hippolyte, queen of the Amazons. (In different versions Hippolyte is known as Antiope.) In one account Theseus carried off the queen to be his bride; an Amazon army attempted to retrieve her and attacked Athens. Under Theseus's leadership the Amazons were conquered in a violent conflict. The Amazon queen stayed with Theseus and in due time bore him a son, whom he named Hippolytus.

Later Theseus abandoned the Amazon queen and married Phaedra, daughter of Minos and sister of Ariadne. By this time Hippolytus had grown into a handsome young man and was devoted to the goddess Artemis. However, Aphrodite, goddess of erotic love, was angry that Hippolytus did not worship her. In her jealousy she caused Phaedra to fall in love with her stepson. He, of course, rejected her advances. Shameful of her passion and fearing that Hippolytus would tell her husband, Phaedra wrote a letter falsely accusing Hippolytus of raping her, and then took her own life. Theseus read the letter and, despite Hippolytus's protests of innocence, prayed to Poseidon for his own son's death. Theseus learned the truth too late and Hippolytus died.

Another myth recounts Theseus's adventures with his companion Peirithous. They decided to find their ideal wives together and went to Sparta to abduct the princess Helen, who was renowned for her beauty. They drew lots to decide who would marry Helen, and Theseus won. However, Helen was too young to marry, and Theseus left her with his mother, Aethra, in Troezen. Next the two friends set off to find a partner for Peirithous, who wanted to make Persephone, queen of Hades, his wife.

When the travelers arrived in the underworld, Hades welcomed them and offered them seats. They accepted his invitation, but the chairs in which they sat would not release them. In one version, the chairs induced forgetfulness: anyone who sat in them could not remember how to leave Hades' realm. While the two friends were stuck in their seats, Helen's brothers Castor and Pollux rescued their sister from Aethra. Theseus and Peirithous remained captive until Heracles arrived in the underworld to complete his last labor many years later. Heracles had to bring Cerberus, the three-headed hound of Hades, back to Eurystheus, king of Mycenae. Heracles was able to prize Theseus from his seat, but he failed to release Peirithous, who remained trapped for eternity.

When Theseus returned to Athens, he discovered that he had lost the kingship to Menestheus, a descendant of an earlier Athenian king. Theseus went into exile on the island of Scyros. There his host Lycomedes, who was a supporter of Menestheus, hurled him to his death from a cliff.

Theseus did not lie in an unmarked grave, however. In 475 BCE Athenian general Cimon (c. 510–c. 451 BCE) found a skeleton on Scyros with huge bones that had been buried with a bronze club. He concluded that the body belonged to Theseus. Legend has it that the burial spot was revealed to Cimon by an eagle that scratched the ground above the grave. He returned to Athens with the skeleton and the club and buried the bones in the center of the city. Athenians were delighted that relics of their greatest hero were returned home. Since Theseus was considered by many as protector of the poor, a sanctuary was made around Theseus's tomb where slaves and poor people could find refuge.

Theseus in drama

In early classical dramas that were largely about other Greek heroes, Theseus's character represented virtues that Athenians believed him to exemplify: generosity, justice, and compassion. In *Heracles* by Euripides (c. 486–c. 406 BCE), Theseus supports Heracles on his deathbed; he promises his friend to uphold his name after his death. In *Suppliant Women,* Euripides again casts Theseus as a

Below: In this 18th-century sculpture by Italian artist Antonio Canova, Theseus is portrayed sitting on the body of the Minotaur.

compassionate hero. In the play Theseus insists that the laws of the gods be respected, and he compels the citizens of Thebes to return the bodies of slain enemies for burial. In *Oedipus at Colonus,* the second play in the trilogy that includes *Oedipus Tyrannus* and *Antigone,* but the last one that Sophocles (c. 496–406 BCE) wrote, Theseus welcomes the aged outcast Oedipus to Athens and restores his abducted daughters to him. At the close of the play, Oedipus leads Theseus to the place where Oedipus will die and entrusts the care of the site to the Athenian leader. According to Sophocles' play, Oedipus becomes a guardian hero of Athens and Theseus becomes a protector of Oedipus's tomb.

Theseus also appears in postclassical literature, most notably in *A Midsummer Night's Dream* by British dramatist William Shakespeare (1564–1616). Although the main action of Shakespeare's play takes place in an enchanted forest outside Athens, the final marriage between Theseus and Hippolyte, the Amazon queen, takes place in Theseus's Athenian palace.

Theseus's myth is a popular subject in ancient and modern art. Depictions of his conquest of the Minotaur adorn many ancient Greek vases and Roman frescoes. Spanish artist Pablo Picasso (1881–1973) had a lifelong interest in bulls as well as in mythology—he painted many versions of the encounter between Theseus and the Minotaur. Italian sculptor Antonio Canova (1757–1822) included a statue of Theseus looking down upon the vanquished Minotaur in his classical collection; the contest also appears in the statuary copies of ancient works in the Tuileries Gardens, Paris.

In ancient Greece, Theseus's exploits were represented on the Treasury of the Athenians in Delphi and on the Hephaesteion in Athens. This temple still overlooks the ancient Agora and was once thought to be dedicated to Theseus; it is now known to have been dedicated to the smith god Hephaestus. To this day a subway stop in Athens is called Theseion for the great Athenian hero.

KARELISA HARTIGAN

Bibliography

Cotterell, Arthur. *Oxford Dictionary of World Mythology.* Oxford: Oxford University Press, 1986.

Euripides, and Paul Roche, trans. *10 Plays.* New York: Signet Classic, 1998.

Howatson, M. C., and Ian Chilvers. *Concise Oxford Companion to Classical Literature.* New York: Oxford University Press, 1993.

SEE ALSO: Amazons; Ariadne; Crete; Daedalus; Dionysus; Heracles; Hippolytus; Minos; Pasiphae; Poseidon; Zeus.

THETIS

Thetis, a Nereid, was the mother of Achilles, the greatest warrior in Greek mythology. Her role in Achilles' story, and in other myths, reveals her as an archetypal mother figure.

The 50 daughters of the sea god Nereus and the sea nymph Doris were known as the Nereids. The beautiful Nereids lived in the Aegean Sea, which they guarded while also protecting sailors from harm. For example, they helped the Greek Argonauts sail safely past

the twin dangers of the monster Scylla and the whirlpool Charybdis on their way back from Colchis, where they had won the Golden Fleece. Thetis was the best known of the Nereids, and was exceptionally beautiful. In addition, like her father Nereus and the sea god Proteus, she had the ability to change shape into whatever she wanted.

Marriage to a mortal

Both Zeus, the king of the gods, and Poseidon, the most powerful sea god, loved Thetis. However, when the goddess Themis foretold that the Nereid would have a son who would be more powerful than his father, they left her alone—neither deity wanted a son who might overthrow him. Instead, the gods decided that Thetis should marry Peleus, king of Phthia in northeast Greece. Thetis, repelled by the idea of marrying a mere mortal, resisted Peleus by changing her shape. However, the king prayed to the gods for help and learned from Proteus that to control Thetis he must hold her tightly, whatever form she took. Peleus heeded this advice and won Thetis's hand in marriage.

Thetis and Peleus's wedding set in motion the chain of events that led to the Trojan War. They invited all the gods and goddesses to the celebration, except for the unpleasant Eris, goddess of discord. Eris turned up regardless and threw a golden apple among the crowd, marked, "To the fairest." The goddesses Aphrodite, Athena, and Hera, each thinking herself the fairest, fought over the apple. Eventually they asked the Trojan prince Paris to judge for them. He chose Aphrodite, who rewarded him with the love of Helen, the most beautiful woman in the world. Helen, however, was already married to the Greek king Menelaus. When Paris ran away with her, the Greeks declared war on Troy.

Thetis and Achilles

Soon after marrying Peleus, Thetis gave birth to their son, Achilles. She loved him dearly and could not bear the thought that, since the child's father was mortal, he might not live forever like her. She also knew that her son was fated to die in battle at Troy, but desperately wanted to

Left: This portrait of Zeus and Thetis was painted by French artist Jean-Auguste-Dominique Ingres (1780–1867).

Above: This painting, by 18th-century French artist Antoine Rogat Borel, depicts Thetis immersing Achilles in the Styx River.

prevent this outcome. Thetis tried to burn away Achilles' mortality in a fire, but she was disrupted by Peleus, who thought she was murdering their child. Furious at her husband's intervention, Thetis returned to live in the sea. In another account, told by Roman poet Statius (45–96 CE), Thetis made Achilles invulnerable by dipping him in the underworld Styx River. The boy retained a weak spot, however: his heel, which his mother had held while dipping him in the water.

Despite her return to the sea, Thetis never stopped watching over her son. When Achilles was nine, the seer Calchas predicted that the Greeks could not win the Trojan War unless Achilles fought with them. So Thetis disguised her son as a girl and took him to the island of Scyros, where she hoped he would be well hidden. Her plan failed: the Greeks discovered him, and Achilles set off for Troy.

Thetis often intervened in the Trojan War to support her son—interventions that were described by Greek poet Homer (c. ninth–eighth century BCE) in his epic the *Iliad*. When Achilles argued with the Greek general Agamemnon and withdrew from the fighting, Thetis persuaded Zeus to give the Trojans the upper hand to teach the general a lesson. As a result of Achilles' refusal to fight, his friend Patroclus went into battle disguised as Achilles, only to be killed by the Trojan Hector. Patroclus's death spurred

Achilles to rejoin the war, but Hector had stolen his armor from his dead companion's body. Thetis went to Hephaestus, the blacksmith of the gods, and asked him to make new armor for her son. Finally, when Achilles was killed by Paris, Thetis and the other Nereids rose out of the sea and came to Troy to mourn him.

Mother figure

Besides being Achilles' doting mother, Thetis cared for other gods and heroes when they needed her. For example, when Hera threw Hephaestus from heaven in her disgust at his lameness, Thetis and the goddess Eurynome rescued him. When Dionysus, god of wine, dived into the sea after being chased by a mortal, Thetis comforted him.

Thetis was an example of a typical character found in myths—the loving mother figure. Her story also explores the concept of destiny and whether it can be altered. Greek mythology contains many instances of people trying to avoid the fate predicted for them, but somehow, as in the case of Achilles, it almost always comes true.

ANNA CLAYBOURNE

Bibliography
Hamilton, Edith. *Mythology*. Boston, MA: Black Bay Books, 1998.
Homer, and Robert Fagles, trans. *The Iliad*. New York: Penguin USA, 2003.

SEE ALSO: Achilles; Dionysus; Helen; Hephaestus; Nereus; Nymphs; Peleus.

THOR

Thor was one of the foremost Norse gods, recognized by Germanic peoples across northern Europe as a fierce warrior deity. To the other gods he offered protection against the giants; to his human worshipers in Scandinavia and elsewhere, he offered a safeguard against evil. Thor was also a god of thunder and lightning, wind and rain, fertility and farming, and laws.

Most Norse people regarded Thor as the son of the chief god, Odin, and the giantess Jörd. His wife was Sif, of whom little is known but who may have been a fertility goddess. At least three children are attributed to Thor: two sons, Magni and Módi, and a daughter, Thrúd. Icelandic scholar Snorri Sturluson (1179–1241 CE) gave a different account of Thor's background, however. In the prologue to his handbook of mythology, the *Prose Edda,* Snorri wrote that Thor was originally "Tror," a prince endowed with supernatural qualities who came from Troy in western Asia. In this account, Tror met a beautiful witch named Sibil, whom Snorri identified as Sif, and with her fathered a race of heroes, including Odin. This race then left Asia and journeyed north to Scandinavia. Snorri was a Christian, and his account—which, incidentally, explains the origin of the word *Aesir* (the collective term for the Norse gods under Odin) as a corruption of *Asia*—may be seen as an attempt to explain pagan gods in Christian terms.

Snorri's description of Thor, however, is one that all ancient Norse people would almost certainly have recognized: he describes him as "the strongest of all the gods and men." Strength and ferocity were two of Thor's chief characteristics. According to the poem *Thrymskvida,* part of the 12th-century *Poetic Edda,* Thor had a bushy red beard and glaring eyes, physical attributes also evident in Viking carvings of the god. Thor was held to be a noisy deity—people thought that thunder was caused by the rattle of his chariot wheels as he drove across the sky. For a god whose main opponents were giants, whom he took great pleasure in smashing with his hammer, many of Thor's own qualities were surprisingly giantlike. His appetite, for instance, was enormous: on one visit to Jotunheim, home of the giants, he ate an entire ox, eight salmon, and other dishes. His self-control, too, was often limited: there are many instances in the myths when the other gods have to restrain Thor from acting on his aggressive impulses. One poem, *Hárbardsljód,* describes a wisdom contest between Thor and Odin in which wily Odin emerges a clear winner. Thor could also be a god of surprises: another poem, *Alvíssmal,* relates how Thor outwitted the dwarf Alvís, whose name means "all-wise."

Thor's possessions

Thor's hall, Bilskírnir, with 540 rooms, was the largest building ever built. His chariot was pulled by his two goats, Tanngnjóst and Tanngrísnir. Thor's most important possessions were a magic belt that doubled his strength whenever he wore it, a pair of iron gloves, and, above all, his mighty hammer, Mjöllnir. This hammer, the use of which required Thor to wear iron gloves, was the Aesir gods' first and last means of defense against their sworn enemies, the giants. It was an awesome weapon since it never missed its target when thrown and always returned to its owner's hands, like a boomerang. One myth suggests that the hammer also had another, greater power: after Thor slaughtered and ate his two goats, he placed their skins on the ground and blessed them with Mjöllnir. The goats immediately sprang to life again.

Thor's wife, Sif, played a small but significant role in the story of how Thor obtained his hammer. The trickster god Loki cut off Sif's golden hair in a fit of mischief. Thor was so angry with Loki that he threatened to kill him. Loki promised that he would make good the damage he had done, and persuaded two skillful dwarfs to make Sif a new head of hair, as well as a spear for Odin and a ship

Right: This illustration of Thor, from a book published in 1911, was painted by British artist Arthur Rackham (1867–1939).

for Frey, the fertility god. He then challenged two more dwarfs to match the craft work of the first two. This competition led to the production of a golden boar for Frey; a magic gold ring, Draupnir, for Odin; and, finally, Thor's hammer.

Thor and Hrungnir

Most of the myths about Thor involve fights with giants. A typical encounter involved Hrungnir, a giant whose head and heart were made of stone. Odin and Hrungnir had a horse race, but at the end of the contest the giant could not stop his mount from crashing through the gates of Asgard, home of the gods. Out of courtesy, the gods invited Hrungnir to join them for a drink and offered him one of Thor's huge goblets. The giant became drunk, and began to proclaim that he would destroy all the gods. In response, the gods called for Thor, who, furious that a giant should be drinking from his goblet, challenged Hrungnir to a fight. The two agreed to have the duel on neutral ground, so Hrungnir returned to Jotunheim to collect his shield and his whetstone. The other giants also made a huge warrior out of clay, named Mist-Calf, to support Hrungnir. Thor's cunning servant Thialfi arrived at the appointed site before his master. He mocked Hrungnir for holding his shield in

Below: This 13th-century smith's mold was used to cast both crucifixes and Thor's hammers—Christianity and paganism coexisted.

Parallel Gods

Thor's role as a thunder god links him to many other ancient storm deities. These include the Greek and Roman kings of the gods, Zeus and Jupiter; Indra, the chief Vedic god of Indian myth; and the Hittite god of storms and thunderbolts. Thor's duels with the Midgard Serpent also link him to some of these gods. Indra slayed the dragon Vritra, who had swallowed the world's waters and caused a drought, while the Hittite storm god's long-standing enemy was the giant serpent Illuyankas. Common themes in these mythologies are not surprising: Norse peoples, Greeks, Romans, Hittites, and Indra-worshiping Indians were all Indo-European peoples, who originated either in central Europe or central Asia before spreading north, south, east, and west. Wherever Indo-Europeans settled, they introduced a tradition of powerful male sky gods.

front of him, telling him that Thor was traveling underground and would strike from below. The giant believed Thialfi's lie and stood on his shield. When Thor arrived he threw his hammer at Hrungnir, who retaliated by hurling his whetstone. The two weapons collided in midair: Thor's smashed through the whetstone and then the giant himself. Meantime, Thialfi killed Mist-Calf. Thor did not escape unharmed, however: a piece of whetstone lodged in his head.

Right: This 19th-century illustration depicts Thor using his hammer, thunder, and lightning in a battle against giants.

Thor and Loki

Thor's relationship with Loki was highly ambivalent. On the one hand, the two were traveling companions, journeying together to confront the giants Thrym, Geirröd, and Utgard-Loki, among others. On the other hand, Loki often went out of his way to make trouble for Thor. He cut off Sif's hair, for example, and persuaded Thor to visit Geirröd unarmed, in order to save himself. The poem *Lokasenna* demonstrates an occasion when Thor came close to killing Loki. Irritated by the trickster's mocking humor, Thor replies: "Shut up, you feeble wretch. My mighty hammer, Mjöllnir, will stop your mouth. With my right hand I'll smash you with Hrungnir's killer so that every bone in your body shatters." One reason Loki was often paired with Thor is that the two complemented each other: Thor provided brute strength, while Loki offered cunning. Yet, in the final reckoning, Loki was no friend of Thor's. Loki would lead the forces of darkness against the gods at Ragnarok, while his son, the Midgard Serpent, would die at Thor's hands only to kill the god with his poison.

Left: This illustration, from an illuminated manuscript, depicts Thor fishing for the Midgard Serpent from a boat belonging to giant Hymir.

Some scholars believe that the origins of this myth lie in religious rituals. The Sami, people of northern Scandinavia, made images of their thunder god in which an iron nail was inserted into the head. Similar to the piece of whetstone in the story, the nail was used to kindle fire in a ritual that reenacted Thor's production of lightning. The use of a clay figure to represent a giant may have formed part of an initiation ritual in which the figure was destroyed. In contrast, the role of the whetstone in Norse myths may have led to the tool's use as a symbol of royalty, since it linked kings with gods.

Thor without his hammer

Two myths describe what happened when Thor was deprived of his hammer. The first relates how shape-shifting Loki, while in the form of a falcon, was caught by the giant Geirröd. Geirröd released Loki only on condition that he bring Thor to the giant's hall without his weapons. Somehow Loki managed to persuade Thor to undertake the mission. On the journey to Jotunheim, however, a friendly giantess named Grith lent the god her own magical belt, iron gloves, and staff. Nearing Geirröd's home, Thor had to cross a huge river, which he did with the help

of Grith's belt—it increased his strength—and her staff. Halfway across, the waters rose when Geirröd's daughter urinated in the river. Thor threw a boulder at the giantess, waded the rest of the way across, and pulled himself onto the bank. When he arrived at Geirröd's court, he was allocated a goat house in which to spend the night. Thor sat down on the one chair in the building, but as soon as he did it began to rise up toward the ceiling, pulled by Geirröd's daughters, who were trying to crush Thor to death. Their plan failed: Thor pushed against the ceiling with his staff and broke their backs. Finally, Thor stepped into Geirröd's hall. As he entered, the giant picked up a red-hot lump of iron and threw it at Thor. Thor caught it with his iron gloves and threw it back, killing the giant.

Another myth tells how Thor's hammer was stolen by the giant Thrym. Thrym would return Mjöllnir to its owner only on one condition: that Thrym be permitted to marry the fertility goddess Freya. She refused outright, so Heimdall, watchman of the gods, proposed that Thor disguise himself as Freya and journey to Thrym's hall in her place. Loki accompanied Thor and, on this occasion, acted for the good of the gods. At the wedding feast Thor astonished the giants with the amount of food and drink he consumed. Loki reassured them that, in her eagerness to meet Thrym, Freya had eaten little for eight whole days. When, on trying to kiss his bride, Thrym remarked that her eyes looked red and angry, Loki replied that in her excitement the goddess had not slept for eight whole nights. At that, Thrym brought out Mjöllnir to bless his marriage. Thor seized his hammer and smashed all the giants present to death.

This myth, recounted in the poem *Thrymskvida,* was comic in intention: effeminate behavior such as cross-dressing was regarded as ridiculous by Norse people, particularly by Vikings. Furthermore, Thor, of all the gods in the pantheon, was usually the most virile and would have been the least likely to impersonate a woman. The satirical nature of the poem has led some scholars to the conclusion that it was unlikely to have been written by anyone who believed in Norse gods. They have suggested that it was probably the work of a Christian writer who made up the tale or embellished an existing story in order to poke fun at the old pagan deities. However, other Indo-European figures were also forced to dress as women during the course of their adventures, most notably the Greek warrior Achilles and the Indian hero Arjuna.

Right: Thor throws his hammer, Mjöllnir, at giant Skrymir. This engraving is by French artist Charles Huard (1875–1965).

Darker myths

Two further myths involving Thor foreshadow the events that Norse people and their gods accepted as inevitable: Ragnarok, the final battle between the gods and the forces of evil. One mysterious tale concerns a visit Thor made with Loki and Thialfi to Jotunheim. Looking for a place to spend the night, they settled on a large building with a wide entrance. Next morning they woke to discover a colossal giant outside—the place where they had slept had been one of his gloves. The giant, whose name was Skrymir, politely asked Thor if he could travel alongside him and his companions. Thor consented. That night, Skrymir's huge snores maddened Thor so much that he struck the giant three times. After each mighty blow of Mjöllnir, however, Skrymir merely rubbed his head and complained that a leaf or an acorn had fallen on him. Skrymir left Thor and the others in the morning, and they resumed their journey. Soon they reached the home of another giant named Utgard-Loki. This giant set the companions to a series of tests, which they all failed. Loki was beaten in an eating contest, Thialfi lost a running race, while Thor failed to drink all the liquid in a drinking horn, was unable to lift the giant's gray cat off the floor, and, finally, was humiliated in a wrestling contest against an old woman. It was only as Thor and his companions were leaving that Utgard-Loki explained exactly how they had been humiliated. Skrymir was Utgard-Loki in disguise—the giant had used sorcery to divert each of Mjöllnir's blows onto a mountain, which now had three deep pits in it. Loki had been beaten by Fire, which consumes everything in its path. Thialfi lost his race to Thought, which moves swifter than anything else. As for Thor, the drinking vessel could not be drained since its tip was in the sea; the gray cat was the huge Midgard Serpent, who lived at the bottom of the ocean; and the old lady who had outwrestled him was none other than Old Age, which eventually overcomes even the strongest opponent.

One interpretation of this myth is that, when the true nature of Thor's challenges was revealed, it emphasized the god's strength. Yet Thor's defeat and humiliation, despite Utgard-Loki's sorcery, were undeniable. They seemed to foreshadow Ragnarok: the gods, for all their power, were not invincible and were destined to fall. The Utgard-Loki myth pits Thor and his companions against harsh reality— fire, thought, and old age—and seems to epitomize the traditionally pessimistic Scandinavian worldview.

A Devoted Follower of Thor

The Icelandic *Eyrbyggja Saga*, thought to have been written between 1230 and 1290 CE, describes a Norwegian chief named Hrolf who was so devoted to the cult of Thor that he became known as Thorolf. Thorolf, in this account, was one of the earliest settlers in Iceland. On his journey from Norway, he took with him the wooden posts that had supported the seat of honor—sacred to Thor—in his ancestral hall. As his ship neared the Icelandic coast, Thorolf threw the posts into the sea and steered the ship in their direction, believing that wherever they landed was where Thor wanted him to settle. The site of Thorolf's landing he duly named Thórsnes, meaning "Thor's Headland."

This was a lost opportunity. Thor would meet the Midgard Serpent again, at the battle of Ragnarok. This time he would kill it, but with a disastrous consequence: poison that came out of the monster's mouth would in turn kill Thor.

Worship of Thor

Just as Thor protected the other gods from the giants, so Scandinavian peoples worshiped him as a protective deity, capable of warding off evil. This role is suggested by carved Viking stones bearing inscriptions such as "Thor hallow these monuments," and "Thor hallow these runes." People honored Thor for a variety of reasons. Inhabitants of Iceland, before their conversion to Christianity around 1000 CE, regarded him as the god of lawmaking. Iceland's annual legal assembly, known as the Althing, always began on a Thursday, the day of the week named for Thor. Sailors looked to Thor for help, believing that he controlled the winds. Indeed, 11th-century German historian Adam of Bremen wrote that Thor controlled the air, thunder and lightning, winds and rainstorms, good weather, and crops. With such responsibilities, it is not surprising that the god was also associated with agriculture and fertility: one ancient fertility custom practiced by farmers was to put small axes— a symbolic variant on Thor's hammer—in seed holes.

The hammer was not Thor's only symbol—others included oak trees and fossilized sea urchins known as thunderstones—but it was the most widespread and potent. References to Thor's hammer in several myths suggest that it played a role in religious rituals. In the myth of the missing hammer, for example, the giant Thrym brings out Mjöllnir to bless the marriage. In another myth, Thor resurrects his two slain goats by raising his hammer. Tiny hammers made of silver or base metal have been discovered in ancient graves throughout Scandinavia. Some of them are attached to loops, suggesting that people wore them

The Midgard Serpent, who appeared in disguise in the Utgard-Loki myth, was Thor's greatest foe. Snorri related a story in which Thor came close to destroying the monster. The god disguised himself as a youth and asked the sea giant Hymir to take him fishing. Hymir agreed, and Thor cut the head off one of the giant's oxen to use as bait. Out at sea, Thor cast his line with the ox's head fastened to a hook. To Hymir's horror, the Midgard Serpent took the bait as Thor revealed himself to the giant, heaving so hard on his line that his feet went through the floor of the boat and struck the seabed. The serpent's head emerged from the sea, but just as Thor was preparing to kill it with his hammer, Hymir cut the line and the monster was saved.

Below: This 12th-century Swedish brooch is decorated with a thunderstone sea urchin, representing Thor, flanked by two animal effigies.

Above: First settled by Norwegian Vikings about 870 CE, Iceland adopted Christianity in 1000.

around their necks as amulets, or charms. Some scholars believe that, during the Viking period (9th to 11th centuries CE), people displayed hammer pendants in direct opposition to Christians, many of whom wore the cross.

Greater than Odin?

There is some anecdotal evidence to suggest that, by the Viking period, worship of Thor had overtaken that of Odin. Traditionally, kings and warriors made up the followers of Odin, god of war. Ordinary people, however, seem to have developed a greater attachment to Thor, a bluff, gruff, and rather human figure, who was also responsible for the things that really mattered in their daily lives—principally the weather and protection from evil. The number of people and places named for Thor hint strongly at his popularity. For men, these names include Thorkel, Thórir, and Thorbjörn; for women, Thóra, Thórdis, and Thorgerd; and for places, Thórsnes (Thor's Headland), Thórshofn (Thor's Haven), and Thorsberg (Thor's Rock). Several accounts describe temples where people worshiped Thor. Adam of Bremen described a great temple at Uppsala, Sweden, in which a statue of Thor stood in the center, with lesser images of Odin

and Frey to the left and right. Danish historian Saxo Grammaticus (c. 1150–after 1216) described another Swedish temple of Thor, which in 1125 had been destroyed by Christians. Saxo Grammaticus wrote that the temple had contained "huge heavy hammers of bronze." However, there is little archaeological evidence to show that Norse people worshiped in temples. Scholars think most rituals were performed outdoors; references to temples were, in all likelihood, Christian interpretations of wooden halls or even houses that may have contained small shrines or statues of the old gods.

ANDREW CAMPBELL

Bibliography

Cotterell, Arthur. *Oxford Dictionary of World Mythology*. New York: Oxford University Press, 1986.

Davidson, H. R. Ellis. *Scandinavian Mythology*. London, England: Hamlyn, 1982.

Littleton, C. Scott, ed. *Mythology: The Illustrated Anthology of World Myth and Storytelling*. San Diego, CA: Thunder Bay Press, 2002.

Orchard, Andy. *Cassell's Dictionary of Norse Myth and Legend*. London: Cassell, 1997.

Warner, Marina, ed. *World of Myths*. London: The British Museum Press, 2003.

SEE ALSO: Aesir; Apocalypse Myths; Dragons; Fertility; Freya; Germanic Peoples; Giants; Greece; Hittites; India; Jupiter; Loki; Natural Forces; Odin; Scandinavia; Thrym; Zeus.

THRYM

Thrym, king of the Norse Frost Giants, lived in a great hall in the mountains at Thrymheim ("Storm home"). He and the giants were notorious for causing violent storms when they were angry, but they could also be loyal, jovial companions.

The figures of Thrym and the Frost Giants arose from an earlier mythic consciousness in which natural forces such as the weather were perceived to be giants—sometimes wildly terrifying and at other times calm. Giants were generally destructive in the Norse texts known as the Eddas, in which they were often portrayed as the Norse gods' stooges. However, when the gods needed to recall the past, they willingly consulted the giants, whose memories were far longer and richer than their own.

Thrym's role in Norse mythology is told in the *Poetic Edda* in a story called *Thrymskvida*. According to this myth Thrym desired only one thing: Freya, goddess of love, as his wife. He set about ensnaring her. He calculated that by stealing Thor's hammer—a weapon that was greatly prized by the Aesir, the most important group of gods in the Norse pantheon—he might be able to bargain for Freya's hand in marriage. The giant king was cunning and was able to steal Thor's hammer while the mighty god slept.

When the chief Norse deity Odin discovered the theft, he sent for the trickster Loki and ordered him to recover the hammer. Loki suspected Thrym was the thief, so he approached Freya to borrow her feathered flying cloak to speed him on his quest, then set off to find Thrym. Loki eventually found him at Thrymheim, busy braiding gold collars for his dogs and tending to his horses.

Loki questioned Thrym about the missing hammer but had not probed too deep before the king laid out his bargain: he would return Thor's hammer if he and Freya could be married. Much relieved by the simplicity of Thrym's demands, Loki returned to Thor, and they went to Freya. On hearing the news, Freya refused Thrym's demands and stormed out of the hall. Freya was the daughter of the giantess Skadi. She belonged to a group of Norse deities called the Vanir who were older than the Aesir. Her anger arose from pride in her lineage and also in her status: According to the myth, Freya was so insulted by the proposal that her neck swelled with rage and the magic necklace of Brísingamen broke. Freya had slept with

Left: Norse love goddess Freya is depicted spinning clouds in this illustration by Helen Stratton (active 1891–1925). In Norse mythology, Thrym was attracted to Freya by her unsurpassed beauty.

Left: Among Viking artifacts archaeologists have discovered in Denmark were this silver ring and this necklace, which bears a pendant in the form of Thor's hammer, Mjöllnir.

four dwarf goldsmiths in exchange for the necklace.

Without Freya, Loki and Thor worried that the hammer was irretrievable. However, Heimdall, watchman of the gods, made a suggestion. He proposed that Thor disguise himself to appear like Freya and then go to Thrym and trick him. Thor was reluctant to pretend, arguing that he was a god and not a goddess, but Loki convinced him to wear the costume and also joined him in disguise as his handmaiden. Dressed as two women, the companions went to Thrymheim to recover the stolen hammer.

A deceitful bride

Thrym was overjoyed when his victims arrived and called for a wedding celebration in honor of his bride, but during a feast to mark the wedding, Thor ate a whole ox and drank three great barrels of mead. Thrym was alarmed. Loki reassured him, saying that Freya was hungry because she had fasted for eight nights in anticipation of the

marriage. Thrym relaxed until he went to kiss his bride and noticed Thor's fiery-red eyes. Shocked, Thrym recoiled and Loki returned with another lie: he told Thrym that his bride had not slept for the past eight nights because of her anxiety about the wedding. Thrym was deceived again and sent for Thor's hammer, Mjöllnir, to be laid in his bride's lap to sanctify the marriage. So that his bride would not wait any longer, Thrym ordered the marriage proceedings to begin. For a moment there was no sound. Then with a roar Thor tore off his bridal veils, snatched up the hammer, and smashed Thrym to death. He also killed other giants who had come to attend the wedding.

Mythographers suggest that this story might preserve echoes of an indigenous Neolithic people's struggle against stronger Indo-Germanic invaders known as the Battle Ax people. The story can also be understood as a metaphor for violent mountain storms that occurred across northern Europe, when thunder and lightning represented the sounds of Thor, Thrym, and the Frost Giants in battle.

Finally, since both names refer to thunder, scholars have suggested that Thrym may have been an earlier form of Thor. This interpretation of the story views Thrym and Thor locked in a power struggle for identity: Thor destroys Thrym in order to assert his power and his superiority in the Norse pantheon. More recent interpretations of the myth suggest that there are various messages contained in the story, including the fact that love cannot be bargained for and weapons are only safe in the right hands.

KATHLEEN JENKS

Thor's Mighty Hammer

Thor's mighty hammer, Mjöllnir ("crusher," "striker"), was crafted by the dwarf Sindri. It never missed its mark and always returned to the hand of the thunder god. It was considered to be a blessing if the hammer was present at a ceremony. Small hammer images were associated with weddings, since people believed a force that could take life could just as powerfully heal and restore the fertility of life. These amulets were worn throughout northern Europe and were a familiar sign of Nordic beliefs, just as the cross would become for Christians.

Bibliography

Hamilton, Edith. *Mythology*. Boston, MA: Black Bay Books, 1998.
Lindow, John. *Norse Mythology: A Guide to the Gods, Heroes, Rituals, and Beliefs*. New York: Oxford University Press, 2002.
Simek, Rudolf, and Angela Hall, trans. *A Dictionary of Northern Mythology*. Rochester, NY: Boydell and Brewer, 1993.

SEE ALSO: Aesir; Freya; Heimdall; Loki; Odin; Thor.

TIAMAT

According to the Babylonian creation story *Enuma Elish,* the goddess Tiamat was the embodiment of the original watery chaos of the universe. She was a gigantic dragonlike creature who personified the saltwater (the ocean) or the "saltwater abyss" at the beginning of time. As the primeval mother, she also represented the forces of disorder and chaos in the universe.

The best-known version of the *Enuma Elish* was written on seven clay tablets in cuneiform (a writing system that used wedge-shaped characters) in the 12th century BCE. The tablets were found in the middle of the 19th century in the ruins of the palace of the Assyrian king Ashurbanipal (reigned 668–627 BCE) in Nineveh—the capital of ancient Assyria (in modern northern Iraq)—and were published soon after.

The first tablet of the *Enuma Elish* introduced the various deities of the pre-creation universe, which was watery and chaotic. Apsu was the god of fresh (sweet) water, and Tiamat was the goddess of salt water. As god of fresh water, Apsu represented the life-giving power of moisture. Tiamat, on the other hand, represented the

Above: In this 1924 illustration by Armenian artist Zabelle C. Boyajian, Marduk is depicted casting his magic nets to ensnare Tiamat.

Above: Part of the story of the creation of the gods Apsu and Tiamat is inscribed on this seventh-century-BCE tablet from Assyria, in northern Iraq.

destructive power of salt water, which kills land plants and provides no refreshment for the thirsty. Everything in the primordial darkness was swirling, but Apsu was regarded as being more controlled, like rain or riverwater, while Tiamat was chaotic and unpredictable, like the ocean.

The first gods come forth

The two waters joined and produced Anshar and Kishar, gods of the horizon. Anshar and Kishar produced Anu, god of sky, who in turn fathered Ea (also known as Enki) by the mother goddess Nammu. Ea married Damkina, who was probably another version of the mother goddess.

While Apsu and Tiamat together represented rest and inertia, the new gods stood for energy and activity. They were too noisy for Apsu, and were disrespectful, too. He planned to destroy all his descendants but was preempted by Ea, who killed his great-grandfather. Ea and Damkina then built their home on Apsu's body—just in time for Damkina to give birth to Marduk.

Marduk, patron god of the city of Babylon, was the god of spring. He was symbolized both by sunlight and lightning. As god of lightning, he was connected with the other storm gods such as Baal. Instead of the chaos and violence of wind and rain, however, Marduk came to represent peace and order.

Tiamat is enraged

Meanwhile, Tiamat had become disturbed by the waves created by the new gods. Although she had counseled Apsu not to kill their offspring, she was enraged at the murder of her husband. She had not helped Apsu when Ea killed him, and was now being reproached for this by the other old gods. Vowing to have revenge, she created 11 monsters—serpents and dragons. Tiamat then took a new husband, Kingu, firstborn of the monsters, and put him in charge of her newly assembled army.

Just as Ea had detected the plans of Apsu, he now realized that Tiamat was preparing to do battle against the young gods. Anshar, god of the horizon, commanded Ea to do something about the planned attack. Ea tried to stop the goddess before she unleashed on the other gods the destructive forces she had assembled, but he was not successful. Anu also attempted to persuade Tiamat not to fight, but failed. The gods concluded that none of them could get close to Tiamat and escape with his life—none, that is, except Marduk.

Ea told his son that it was his destiny to overthrow Tiamat. Marduk replied that he would be happy to overthrow the apparently unstoppable monster, provided his conditions were met. These were that he would become ruler of all the gods and head of the pantheon over Anu.

The council of the gods tested Marduk's powers by asking him to conjure up a garment, destroy it, and then bring it back. After he passed the test, the council enthroned Marduk as high king and supreme commander. In addition, they gave him powerful magical weapons: a club, a net, bow and arrows, and seven destructive storm winds. These winds were the evil wind, whirlwind, dust storm, four wind, seven wind, cyclone, and irresistible wind.

Marduk's battle with Tiamat

When they first saw Tiamat, Marduk and his helpers were awestruck and afraid. Marduk recovered quickly, however, and raised a fierce storm. After entangling Tiamat in a net, he unleashed the evil wind. When she opened her mouth to devour him, the evil wind inflated Tiamat and she was rendered helpless. While his opponent was incapacitated, Marduk killed her with an arrow, splitting her belly. He captured the other gods and monsters who were her allies, and took the tablets of fate (destiny) that Kingu had held and gave them to Anu.

After smashing Tiamat's head with a club, Marduk split her dead body in half. He made one half into the sky and the other into the earth. Marduk arranged the stars and other heavenly bodies and then turned his attention to the land. Using some dust created by his grandfather, Anu, he proceeded to mold the landscape of the earth. Tiamat's head became a mountain, with two streams of water running from her eyes. These streams were the Tigris and Euphrates rivers, which gave Mesopotamia its name in Roman times—"Land between the rivers." The goddess's nostrils became lakes and her breasts were hills. Marduk tied her dragon's tail in a knot and used it as a plug to keep the waters of Apsu from flooding the world. Although the waters of the abyss needed to be controlled, some moisture was required on the earth, so Marduk created rain for the earth from the spittle of Tiamat.

The Creation of the Heavens

Marduk built dwelling places for the other gods in the heavens. As they took their places, they established the days and months and seasons of the year. The homes of the gods were the constellations, especially those of the zodiac. These 12 signs made up the 12 months of the year. The phases of the moon determined the cycles of the months, creating the calendar that we still use today.

The sky also had barriers to keep back the waters of chaos. Marduk measured Apsu, the watery world where he was born, and created the Esharra, an area in the sky of equal size. This would become the dwelling place of Anu, Ea, and the other gods.

Above: The Tigris River, one of two great rivers that borders Mesopotamia, was said to flow from Tiamat's eye.

The gods punished Kingu by tying him up and slashing his arteries. From the blood of Kingu, mixed with dust from the earth, the gods created humans, who were intended to work for the gods. Thus, according to the Babylonian myth, a little bit of Tiamat, monster of the saltwater abyss, flows through the veins of all humans.

A Babylonian protagonist

Like the Assyrians before them, the Babylonians ruled a vast empire in southwestern Asia. Both the Assyrian and Babylonian cultures absorbed many elements, particularly religion and mythology, from the older Sumerian civilization (Sumeria was located in the southern part of what is today Iraq). The Sumerian myths and gods were integrated with the pantheons of the various groups that followed, including the Akkadians, Assyrians, and Babylonians. Tiamat, however, appears only in the Babylonian version of the creation stories.

LYN GREEN

Bibliography

Black, Jeremy, and Anthony Green. *Gods, Demons, and Symbols of Ancient Mesopotamia: An Illustrated Dictionary.* Austin, TX: University of Texas Press, 1992.

McCall, Henrietta. *Mesopotamian Myths.* Austin, TX: University of Texas Press, 1992.

Oates, Joan. *Babylon.* New York: Thames and Hudson, 1986.

SEE ALSO: Baal; Calendars; Creation Myths; Enki; Enlil; Marduk; Mesopotamia.

TIRESIAS

In Greek mythology, Tiresias was a soothsayer—someone who could predict the future. He was famous around ancient Greece, and people would often travel great distances to seek his advice. He was known for being blind, living to a great age, and repeatedly changing his gender.

Tiresias was the son of Everes, a shepherd, and the nymph Chariclo. He is said to have had three daughters: Manto, Historis, and Daphne. Tiresias lived in Thebes, a great city near Athens. Part human and part divine, he lived to a much greater age than any normal human being. Some sources say he lived for seven generations, which would total more than 150 years. Others say that he lived for nine generations, or up to 200 years.

Tiresias's blindness

There are several different accounts of the cause of Tiresias's blindness. Some say that Tiresias was such a skilled soothsayer that he was able to give away all the gods' plans and secrets to humans, and that the gods blinded him as a punishment. In another version, he was blinded after accidentally seeing the goddess Athena taking a bath. In some accounts Athena blinded him; in others it was the work of the Titan Cronus, who inflicted blindness on any mortal who looked upon a deity without the god's consent. Tiresias's mother, Chariclo, begged Athena to give her son back his sight, but Athena was unable to do this, so she gave Tiresias a different kind of vision—the gift of prophecy. She also granted him the power to understand

the language of birds, guaranteed him a long life, and said that he would still be able to predict the future after his death, when he went to the underworld.

Changing gender

According to a different myth about Tiresias, one day he came across two snakes mating. He hit them with a stick, killing the female snake. At that moment he was transformed into a woman. Tiresias remained a woman for the next seven years, during which time he got married. At the end of the seven years, he again saw two snakes mating and hit them with a stick. This time the male snake died, and Tiresias became a man again.

Sometime after this, Zeus, the chief Greek god, quarreled with his wife, Hera, about the joys of love and

Right: In this fifth-century-BCE vase painting, Greek hero Odysseus consults the standing soothsayer, Tiresias. In Greek mythology Odysseus sought Tiresias's advice to help him return to his home and to his wife.

whether they were better for a man or for a woman. Hera said they must be better for men, which was why Zeus had so many affairs. Zeus said that women had a better time. Since Tiresias had experienced life as a man and as a woman, Zeus and Hera asked him to settle the dispute. Tiresias declared that Zeus was correct, saying that women experience nine or 10 times the amount of pleasure making love than men do. Hera was so furious about losing the argument that she struck Tiresias blind, but Zeus rewarded him by giving him the power to see into the future.

Tiresias and Thebes

Tiresias often helped and advised the people of Thebes. Most famously of all, he revealed to Oedipus, king of Thebes, that he had unknowingly killed his own father and married his own mother. Horrified at the news,

Below: Tiresias, the blind soothsayer, is depicted with a helpful boy in this 18th-century illustration by British artist John Flaxman (1755–1826).

Oedipus blinded himself and ran away from Thebes in despair, leaving the city in trouble. The citizens were suffering from a deadly plague, Oedipus's sons were fighting for the throne, and the city was under attack by invaders. Tiresias declared that the end of the plague would come when a Theban man sacrificed himself. Menoeceus, Oedipus's cousin, killed himself to fulfill the prophecy. However, the city was still plagued, and Tiresias said that the citizens should flee. They did so, eventually coming to a cold spring called Tilphussa. Tiresias is reported to have died after drinking from the waters of the spring.

In the underworld

In the *Odyssey* by Homer (c. ninth–eighth century BCE)—the tale of Odysseus's long journey home from the Trojan War—the enchantress Circe tells Odysseus that he must visit Tiresias in the Land of the Dead and ask him about the future. In the underworld, Tiresias tells Odysseus that he will find the Island of the Sun, and that if he wants to get home quickly he must not harm the magical sheep and cattle that graze there, since they belong to the sun god Helios. However, Odysseus's ships become stranded at the island, and his men cannot resist killing some of the animals to eat. As Tiresias had predicted, Odysseus arrives home 10 years late and alone, after all his men had been killed and his ships wrecked.

Enduring appeal

Tiresias was a well-known character in the ancient world. He was considered to be the greatest and wisest of all soothsayers. Ancient writers who recalled Tiresias's life included Aeschylus (525–456 BCE), Pindar (c. 522–c. 438 BCE), Sophocles (c. 496–406 BCE), Euripides (c. 486–c. 406 BCE), Apollodorus (third century BCE), Hyginus (first century BCE), and Ovid (43 BCE–17 CE). Since then, Tiresias has continued to appear in literature and art. Victorian poets Alfred Lord Tennyson (1809–1892) and A. C. Swinburne (1837–1909) both wrote poems about him, and more famously he appeared as a character in the epic poem *The Waste Land* by T. S. Eliot (1888–1965).

ANNA CLAYBOURNE

Bibliography

Homer, and Robert Fagles, trans. *The Odyssey*. New York: Penguin USA, 1999.

Ovid, and A. D. Melville, trans. *Metamorphoses*. New York: Oxford University Press, 1998.

SEE ALSO: Athena; Cronus; Daphne; Hera; Odysseus; Oedipus.

TITANS

In Greek mythology the Titans were the first generation of gods to come into being after the creation of the basic features of the cosmos. For a time they ruled the universe. However, they were ultimately overthrown by their successors, the Olympians.

According to Greek poet Hesiod (fl. 800 BCE), who wrote an account of the origins of the universe in his epic poem *Theogony*, the first entity to come into being was Chaos, a great void into which all matter would subsequently be fitted. It was followed by Gaia (the earth), Eros (love), and Tartarus. Tartarus was a dark place located far beneath the earth that would later serve as a great prison for gods and other immortal beings who could not be killed. Gaia, who was personified as a goddess, then gave birth to Pontus (the oceans), Ourea (the mountains), and Uranus (the sky). After she had created the basic physical characteristics of the world, Gaia then mated with Uranus to create a whole generation of actual beings. These were the 12 Titans and six monsters: the three Cyclopes and the three Hecatoncheires (or Hundred-Handed Ones). The Cyclopes were one-eyed giants, while the Hecatoncheires were creatures with 50 heads and 50 pairs of arms each. There were six male and six female Titans. In order of birth, the brothers were Oceanus, Coeus, Crius, Hyperion, Iapetus, and Cronus; the sisters were Theia, Rhea, Themis, Mnemosyne, Phoebe, and Tethys. Some of the offspring of the first generation were also generally considered as belonging to the Titans, in particular Prometheus, son of Hyperion, and Atlas, son of Iapetus.

The overthrow of Uranus

Uranus, the first ruler of the world, was a cruel king and a jealous father. He prevented his children from being born, forcing them back into the depths of Gaia's womb. Gaia was appalled by this, so she created a sickle made of adamant (an unbreakable stone, often identified with diamond) and suggested to her children that they punish Uranus for his outrageous behavior. All were too frightened to speak, with the exception of the youngest son, Cronus, who offered his help.

Cronus and Gaia set up an ambush for Uranus as he returned to Gaia as usual at nightfall. While Uranus lay on Gaia, Cronus came out from hiding and

Right: Titan *by Italian sculptor Alessandro Algardi (1595–1654). The statue depicts a Titan cowering under one of the boulders hurled by the Hecatoncheires.*

1373

castrated his father with the sickle, tossing his testicles into the sea. From the blood spilled during this act, the Giants were born.

As a result of this uprising, the Titans became rulers of the universe. From them came all subsequent generations of gods. The most important of the Titans' offspring were the children of Cronus and Rhea, a group of gods that would later be known as the Olympians, after their home on Mount Olympus.

The Olympians had a troubled entry into the world. Cronus proved to be just as bad a father as Uranus had been. Whenever Rhea gave birth to a child, Cronus swallowed the infant whole. He did this because he feared that one of his children would overthrow him, just as he had overthrown his own father. Finally, Rhea gave birth to Zeus, whom she hid from Cronus. The child grew up in hiding on the island of Crete. When Zeus reached maturity, he conspired with his mother, Rhea, and his grandmother, Gaia, and together they gave Cronus a potion that forced him to disgorge all the children he had swallowed.

The Titanomachia

After he had been reunited with his brothers and sisters—the gods Hades and Poseidon and the goddesses Hera, Demeter, and Hestia—Zeus led the Olympians in a great battle against Cronus and the other Titans to determine who would rule the universe. All but two of the Titans fought against the Olympians:

Right: Titan Struck by Lightning *by French sculptor François Dumont (1688–1726). Zeus's thunderbolts were important weapons in the battle between the Titans and the Olympians.*

only Oceanus and Prometheus joined the side of Zeus. The clash, known as the Titanomachia, lasted for 10 years. The two sides were evenly matched, but the tide of the war turned in favor of the Olympians when Zeus enlisted the help of the Cyclopes and the Hecatoncheires, who had been imprisoned in Tartarus by Cronus. Zeus killed Campe, the monster that guarded these creatures, and freed them. In gratitude both the Cyclopes and the Hecatoncheires joined the war on the side of Zeus. The Hecatoncheires used their great strength to hurl huge boulders at the Titans. The Cyclopes, meanwhile, helped the Olympians by making a trident for Poseidon, a cap of invisibility for Hades, and thunder and lightning for Zeus. The Olympians used these gifts in their struggle and eventually vanquished the Titans.

All but one of the Titans who had fought against Zeus were banished to Tartarus, where they were confined for the rest of eternity. The sole exception was Atlas,

Above: Fall of the Titans *by Peter Paul Rubens (1577–1640) depicts the final stages of the Titanomachia.*

whose special punishment was to hold up the heavens on his shoulders. The punishment inflicted on the Titans greatly angered Gaia, who persuaded the Giants to rise up against the Olympians. The result was another mighty conflict, the Gigantomachia, which the Olympians won only with the help of the mortal hero Heracles.

The ancient Greeks saw the Titanomachia and the Gigantomachia as two stages of the same struggle, a conflict between modern forces of order and an old regime of a more brutal, primitive, and disorderly kind. It is characteristic of the difference between the Titans and the Olympians that a key element in the defeat of Cronus and the Titans was cunning and intelligence. When Cronus demanded his latest newborn child from Rhea, she deceived him by handing him a rock wrapped in swaddling clothes. Similarly, Cronus was tricked into drinking the potion that brought all his children back into the world. The defeat of Cronus was thus a triumph of subtlety and cunning over brute force and ignorance.

Mounts Olympus and Othrys

According to Hesiod, when the battle took place between the Titans and the gods, the two sides were based on different mountains. The Titans lived on Mount Othrys, while Zeus and his siblings dwelled on Mount Olympus. Both mountains are real. Olympus is situated in northern Greece, just west of the Gulf of Thérmai, while Othrys lies around 75 miles to the south. Of the two mountains, Olympus is by far the higher. It stands at 9,570 feet (2,917 m). By contrast, Othrys is only 5,663 feet (1,726 m) high.

The ancient Greeks believed that Mount Olympus was at the center of their country, which was, in turn, at the center of the world. Because Olympus seemed to reach the clouds, the Greeks equated its summit with heaven. According to Greek epic poet Homer (c. ninth–eighth century BCE), "many-peaked Olympus" was in a state of perpetual calm, undisturbed by storms or rain. The chief gods and goddesses met there to settle the affairs of humans. Each of the main Greek gods and goddesses was assigned a dwelling place along Olympus's slopes.

Children of the Titans

Right: This marble statue from the third century BCE depicts the Titan Themis, who was the mother of both the Horae (the seasons) and the Moirai (the Fates).

Among them, the 12 Titans produced thousands of offspring. Many of them were important figures in Greek mythology in their own right. Iapetus, for example, was the father of Prometheus, Epimetheus, and Atlas. Prometheus gave humankind the gift of fire, while Epimetheus was responsible for introducing sorrow and disease to the world by accepting from Zeus the gift of the woman Pandora. As a punishment for his part in the Titanomachia, Atlas was condemned to carry the weight of the heavens on his shoulders for eternity. The descendants of Epimetheus and Prometheus also played significant roles in Greek myth. Deucalion, son of Prometheus, and Pyrrha, daughter of Epimetheus, were the only humans to survive the great flood, and were thus the ancestors of the entire human race. Their son Hellen was the first Greek.

Other Titans were the ancestors of major natural phenomena. Oceanus, the oldest of the Titans, was father of 3,000 river gods and 3,000 water nymphs. All of the major rivers of Greece were said to be his sons. Crius was the grandfather of the four winds: Zephyrus, Boreas, Notus, and Eurus; while Hyperion married his sister Theia to produce the sun god Helios, the moon goddess Selene, and Eos, goddess of the dawn. Two of the female Titans mated with Zeus to produce other important phenomena: Themis gave birth to both the Horae (the seasons) and the Moirai (the Fates), while Mnemosyne (Memory) begat the nine Muses.

The Titanomachia in art

The Titanomachia and the Gigantomachia were represented on numerous monuments in Greece. An important example was the gold and ivory statue of Athena, sculpted by Phidias (fl. c. 490–430 BCE), which stood inside the Parthenon on the Acropolis in Athens. The Gigantomachia was represented on the inside of the warrior goddess's great shield. Also depicted in this work were the battle fought by the Olympians against the Amazons (the Amazonomachia), an image of which was carved on the outside of the shield, and the Olympians' battle against the centaurs (the Centauromachia), which appeared on the goddess's sandals. Like the Titans and Giants, the Amazons and the centaurs were forces of disorder. Thus they were threats to both the Olympian regime and the human world. Depictions of the Titanomachia and the Gigantomachia frequently featured the goddess Athena. An illustration of Athena fighting in the wars featured prominently on versions of a famous robe that were woven every four years and paraded through the streets of Athens as part of her great city festival, the Panathenaia.

Above: Battling Titans *by sculptor Ignác Platzer (1717–1787). The statue stands at the entrance to Prague Castle in the Czech Republic.*

Zagreus and the Titans

One famous myth involving the Titans is the story of the young god Zagreus, who was slain and dismembered by them and later reborn as the Olympian deity Dionysus. Zagreus was worshiped by the adherents of the mystery cult Orphism. The main source for Zagreus's story is the *Dionysiaca*, an epic poem written in the fifth century CE by Nonnus, a Greek writer who lived in Panopolis, Egypt.

During the Titanomachia the goddess Demeter hid her daughter Persephone in a cave for safety. However, she was found by Zeus, who took the form of a snake and raped her. Persephone became pregnant and later gave birth to a son, Zagreus. The infant son of Zeus immediately took his place on his father's throne and began to play with Zeus's thunderbolts. However, Zeus's wife, Hera, was consumed with jealousy and persuaded the Titans to kill Zagreus.

Disguising their faces with chalk, the Titans came to Mount Olympus and attacked the child. Zagreus responded by changing into many different shapes, taking on the appearance of his father Zeus, the Titan Cronus, a newborn baby, a lion, and a bull. However, these efforts could not save him. The Titans killed the infant, cut his body to shreds, and ate the pieces. One part of Zagreus's body remained, however: the heart. Zeus took it and turned it into a potion, which he gave to his mortal lover Semele. Semele drank the potion and in due course became pregnant. Zagreus was thus born again, this time as the god of wine, Dionysus.

In a slight variation on the usual account of the Titanomachia, the Orphics believed that Zeus then struck the Titans with his thunderbolts, turning them to dust. Humankind was created from the ashes. According to Orphic mythology, this accounted for the good and evil that was present in every human being. The evil was derived from the ashes of the bodies of the wicked Titans, while the good came from the remnants of the body of Zagreus that they had eaten.

Another famous depiction of the struggles was found in Pergamon, a city in Asia Minor (part of modern Turkey). There, King Eumenes II (ruled c. 197–c. 160 BCE) built the Altar of Zeus, a monument to national pride and Pergamene achievement. The friezes that decorated the altar depicted the deeds of Telephus, the mythic founder of the city, and the great battles of the Titanomachia and the Gigantomachia. Here again the Titans and Giants symbolized disruption and disorder, standing in contrast to their successors, the Olympian gods, who represented power, success, and civilization.

Etymology and significance

Scholars are divided as to the derivation of the name *Titan*. Some believe it comes from the Greek verb *titaino*, meaning "to stretch" or "to strain," because the Titans had to exert themselves so much in order to overthrow Uranus. Other accounts, however, suggest that the word *Titan* comes from the verb *tino*, meaning "to punish," because the Titans punished the wickedness of their father and would themselves be punished in turn.

At one time, many historians believed that the Titans were the gods of the peoples who lived in the Balkan Peninsula before the Greek-speaking Indo-Europeans migrated there. According to this theory, the Titanomachia could be seen as a mythic account of how the Olympian gods of the Greeks took over from the pre-Greek Titans. This interpretation has largely been rejected, however. An almost identical sequence of events has been identified in the mythologies of other parts of the Mediterranean and western Asia. It seems likely that the similarities are due to the fact that Greek culture was profoundly influenced by contacts with Mesopotamian culture.

In modern English the noun *titan* and the adjective *titanic* have come to be used to describe almost anything that is exceptionally large or overpowering. Hence, what was in its time the largest passenger steamship ever built was named *Titanic*. *Titan* is also the name given to an important series of U.S. rockets, some of which have been used to power NASA's space probes. The largest moon of the planet Saturn, meanwhile, is also called Titan. A number of Saturn's other large moons—Tethys, Rhea, Iapetus, Hyperion, and Phoebe—are named for individual members of the first generation of Titans, while three of Saturn's smaller moons—Atlas, Prometheus, and Epimetheus—are named for members of the next generation of Titans.

ANTHONY BULLOCH

Bibliography

Graves, Robert. *The Greek Myths*. New York: Penguin USA, 1993.

Hesiod, and M. L. West, trans. *Theogony; and Works and Days*. New York: Oxford University Press, 1999.

SEE ALSO: Atlas; Cronus; Cyclopes; Dionysus; Gaia; Giants; Mnemosyne; Oceanus; Prometheus; Uranus; Zeus.

TITHONUS

In Greek mythology, Tithonus was the beautiful son of Laomedon and Strymo, daughter of the Scamander River. His brother was Priam, king of Troy. He was beloved by Eos, goddess of dawn. It was through her that Tithonus achieved immortality, but not eternal youth. Thus, he withered as he grew old and was eventually turned into a cicada, a loud chirping insect.

In his youth, Tithonus was so good-looking that he attracted the amorous attentions of Eos, goddess of dawn, and she carried him off to be her lover. He fathered two children by her—Memnon and Emathion. The abduction of mortals by deities for sexual purposes is a common theme in Greek mythology. Usually, the gods have their way with the humans and then abandon them immediately. Eos herself, for example, had other liaisons at various times with the humans Cleitos and Orion, and she attempted another with Cephalus, but these were no more than brief encounters. The goddess's love for Tithonus was more enduring than any of the others. It survived until Tithonus grew old and his hair turned white. At this point, Eos finally left him, but even then she let him remain in her palace. There he continued to feed on ambrosia (the food of the gods) and wear celestial clothing. At length, however, Tithonus lost the use of his limbs, and Eos then shut him up in his bedchamber, from which his feeble voice could still be heard from time to time.

Ill-chosen words

If nature had been left to take its course, Tithonus would have died. While he was shut away, however, Eos had carried off another mortal, the beautiful boy Ganymede. Zeus wanted this youth for himself, to serve as cupbearer to the gods on Mount Olympus. Although Eos had to submit to the chief god's will, she was entitled to ask him to compensate her for the loss of Ganymede. Her request was that Tithonus be made immortal. Zeus granted her wish to the letter, but unfortunately she had phrased it badly. Eos had demanded only that her lover be given eternal life; she had not said anything about eternal youth, or even about arresting the rate of his physical decay. Thus Tithonus was trapped forever in his disintegrating body. He became more and more decrepit and wizened until Eos finally took pity on him and turned him into a cicada. The insect endlessly croaked his one remaining desire—to be allowed to die. This story is one of the oldest in Greek mythology—parts of it were recounted by poet

Left: The painting on this amphora from the second century BCE shows Eos weeping over the body of her son, Memnon.

Above: To ancient Greeks, dawn was the goddess Eos. Her consort was Tithonus, a mortal to whom she gave the unwanted gift of immortality.

Homer (c. ninth–eighth century BCE). The chirruping noise made by Tithonus after he was turned into a cicada is thought to have been the "unquenched voice" referred to in the "Homeric Hymn to Aphrodite," a poem from the sixth century BCE.

Children of Tithonus

Memnon grew up to become king of the Ethiopians. He dwelled in Africa until the start of the Trojan War, when he promptly answered the call to assist his father's kinsmen. His uncle, King Priam, received him with great honors, and listened attentively as Memnon recounted a series of vivid stories about life in Ethiopia. Only a day after his arrival, however, Memnon grew tired of reminiscence, became impatient for action, and led his troops into the field. He slew Antilochus, son of Nestor, and the Greek forces broke up in disarray until their champion, Achilles, entered the fray and faced Memnon in single combat. The battle between the two men was long and hard, but eventually the Greek prevailed and Memnon was killed. The Trojans fled the scene. Eos, who had looked on helplessly from the heavens as her son was slain, then sent winds to carry his body to the banks of the Esepus River in Paphlagonia, an ancient region of northern Anatolia (part of modern Turkey). In the evening the goddess traveled there and mourned her son. In another version of the story, Memnon's body was wafted back to Ethiopia, where mourners raised his tomb in the grove of the nymphs near a stream. Zeus then turned the sparks and

Right: This engraving by French artist Bernard Picart (1673–1733) depicts Tithonus turning into a cicada. His lover, Eos, looks on helplessly—she condemned him to eternal life.

cinders of Memnon's funeral pyre into birds. The creatures divided into two flocks that fought each other for the pile of ashes until they fell into the flames and were burned as sacrificial victims. Every year thereafter, on the anniversary of Memnon's death, other flocks of birds returned to the scene and fought to their deaths.

Eos was inconsolable over the loss of her son. Her endless tears could be seen early in the morning in the form of dewdrops on the grass. At a certain location on the banks of the Nile River in Egypt stood a great statue of Memnon. According to legend, when the first rays of the rising sun fell on this effigy, it emitted a mournful sound like the snapping of a harp string.

Emathion, the other son of Tithonus and Eos, became king of Arabia. He was killed by Heracles during the hero's 11th labor, the recovery of the golden apples from the garden of the Hesperides. Emathion's offspring became rulers of Macedon, so he was thus one of the mythical ancestors of Alexander the Great (356–323 BCE).

Literary links

The story of Tithonus has inspired many artists and writers since classical antiquity. Of the ancient authors who covered the topic, the most famous was Roman poet Ovid (47 BCE–17 CE) in the *Metamorphoses*. One of the best-known quotations in English literature—"And after many a summer dies the swan"—comes from the poem "Tithonus" by Alfred Lord Tennyson (1809–1892). In this work the eponymous hero laments his fate, saying sadly of himself: "Me only cruel immortality consumes."

JAMES M. REDFIELD

Bibliography

Bulfinch, Thomas. *Bulfinch's Mythology.* New York: Modern Library, 1998.

Homer, and Robert Fagles, trans. *The Iliad.* New York: Penguin USA, 2003.

Howatson, M. C., and Ian Chilvers. *Concise Oxford Companion to Classical Literature.* New York: Oxford University Press, 1993.

Ovid, and A. D. Melville, trans. *Metamorphoses.* New York: Oxford University Press, 1998.

Tennyson, Alfred, and Christopher Ricks, ed. *A Collection of Poems by Alfred Tennyson.* Garden City, NY: International Collectors Library, 1972.

SEE ALSO: Achilles; Eos; Ganymede; Heracles; Laomedon; Memnon; Priam; Zeus.

TLALOC

Tlaloc was worshiped by the Aztecs as a god of rain and fertility. He could bring drought, floods, and disease, as well as new life. Tlaloc was an ancient god of Mesoamerica (Mexico and Central America) whom the Aztecs incorporated into their pantheon to add legitimacy to their empire.

In Aztec myth, Tlaloc belonged to the second generation of gods. The first generation—which comprised Xipe Totec, god of agriculture; Tezcatlipoca, the malevolent creator god; Quetzalcoatl, the feathered-serpent deity; and Huitzilopochtli, protector of the Aztec people—was created by the supreme being Ometeotl. These gods, in turn, created fire, the first man and woman, and the gods of rain and water. Tlaloc, the chief of these water deities, was an immensely powerful divinity. He controlled rain, clouds, thunder, lightning, hurricanes, and mountain springs, as well as a host of lesser deities, known as the Tlaloques, who served as his attendants. Some accounts describe many Tlaloques, while others mention only four or five such beings. Each was responsible for a different type of rain; beneficial rain; fungus rain; windy rain; fiery rain: which may have symbolized drought; and flint-blade rain, which may have symbolized hailstorms.

Tlaloc's control over water meant that he acquired other roles as well. He could help or hinder agriculture by sending the right amount of rain, too much, or too little. This power connected him with fertility, as well as with drought and hunger. Tlaloc and his Tlaloques were also thought to bring diseases that the Aztecs associated with rain and cold winds, including dropsy, leprosy, and rheumatism. Tlaloc's importance was directly linked to the extremes of the Mexican climate, which has long seasons of torrential rain followed by intensely dry seasons. These conditions could inspire uncertainty in the minds of farmers and other people, and increase their desire to appease the rain god. Yet there was another, gentler aspect of Tlaloc. The Aztecs believed that people killed as a result of his power—whether struck dead by lightning, stricken by illness, or drowned—went to the god's paradise of Tlalocan, where they lived in eternal bliss.

Tlaloc had a distinctive appearance and set of sacred symbols. Carved figurines, and written descriptions in Aztec sources, depict him with round, saucerlike eyes and a pronounced upper lip with jaguarlike teeth. Some scholars believe that the jaguar connection derived from the idea that the animal's snarl resembled the rumble of thunder. Tlaloc's possessions were a jade tomahawk, which symbolized a thunderbolt; a writhing serpent, which symbolized lightning; and a jug, from which he poured the rain. The god was also closely associated with mountains: clouds that settled on mountaintops were regarded as a sign of his presence. The Aztecs believed that Tlaloc lived on a mountain to the east of their city of Tenochtitlán (modern Mexico City), which to this day is known as Mount Tlaloc.

Ruler of the third age

Tlaloc's most important role in Aztec myth was as ruler of the third age of the world. The Aztecs believed that the age in which they lived, presided over by the sun god Tonatiuh, was the fifth; before it four different gods had ruled four different races of people, all of whom had been destroyed either because of their own failings or because of wars between the gods, notably battles between Tezcatlipoca and Quetzalcoatl. Tezcatlipoca ruled the first age, when the world was populated by giants. Quetzalcoatl destroyed this age, however, and presided over the next, whose simple people survived by eating seeds of the mesquite tree. Tezcatlipoca, in turn, ended this age by sending an immense wind, the survivors of which were transformed into monkeys. The third age was that of Tlaloc, under whose rule people discovered farming and began to cultivate grain. Quetzalcoatl brought this era to a violent close: he sent a rain of fire, which reduced the world to

Right: This painting of Tlaloc dates from the 13th century CE and comes from the temple at Teotihuacán in modern Mexico. This sacred Aztec site was reconstructed by modern archaeologists.

Aztec Worship

Aztec people incorporated Tlaloc into their own pantheon to legitimize their empire. The Aztecs are thought to have come from the north and settled in the Valley of Mexico, where they built the city of Tenochtitlán in 1325. The city's most important temple, the Teocalli (Great Temple), contained two sanctuaries, the northern one dedicated to Tlaloc and the southern one honoring Huitzilopochtli. Situating both gods in a single temple, which the Aztecs held to be the center of the universe, was a highly symbolic act. It connected the Aztecs and their own protector god Huitzilopochtli to the history and cultures of Mesoamerica through the ancient figure of Tlaloc. The two gods also represented the two primary means by which the Aztecs acquired and maintained their power: warfare, the preserve of Huitzilopochtli, and agriculture, indelibly linked to Tlaloc.

Worship of Tlaloc was a major part of Aztec religion. Five months out of the Aztecs' 18-month ritual year were devoted to Tlaloc and other deities of aquatic life and plants, including his wife Chalchiuhtlicue, the Tlaloques, and salt goddess Uixtocihuatl. These divinities—and, especially, Tlaloc—were commemorated in festivals and rituals such as ceremonial bathing and child sacrifice. Blood and life sacrifices were at the core of Aztec beliefs, stemming from the idea that humans owed blood and lives to the gods, who had sacrificed their own blood when creating the world. This give-and-take relationship with the gods can be seen directly with Tlaloc—people understood that the price for his life-enhancing waters, which provided crops and thus nourishment, was death, in the form of child sacrifice. Remarkable evidence of child sacrifice to the rain god was discovered during excavations of the Teocalli in Mexico City between 1978 and 1982. Among statues of Tlaloc, archaeologists discovered 42 child skeletons, which have been dated to 1454, the year of a great drought in Mexico. Scholars have suggested that these sacrifices were an attempt by the Aztecs to appease Tlaloc, whose rains they beseeched to fall on the parched earth.

Above: These sculptures on a wall of the temple Teocalli in Tenochtitlán depict repeated motifs of the rain god Chac, a deity similar to Tlaloc.

ash and turned people into turkeys. Tlaloc's wife, the water goddess Chalchiuhtlicue, presided over the fourth age, before she destroyed it with a great flood. This flood again transformed the people of the world. This time they became fish.

Attendant Tlaloques

Tlaloc's attendants, the Tlaloques, played an important part in the myth of how the people of the fifth world obtained corn. Quetzalcoatl discovered corn from the ants and, transforming himself into a black ant, found

an enormous store of it in a chamber deep inside a mountain called Tonacatepetl. The other gods decided that humans would need all the food in the mountain if they were to become healthy and strong. Quetzalcoatl tried to move the mountain on his own, but it was too heavy. The other gods then agreed that the diseased god Nanauatzin should split the mountain open. Once this was done, the Tlaloques had the task of gathering up all the corn and scattering it over the four corners of the earth. Consequently, the Aztecs honored Tlaloc's helpers as the deities who had brought corn to humankind.

It is possible that Tlaloc is also the central figure in the legend of how Tezcatlipoca and Quetzalcoatl created the fifth world by ripping the sea monster Tlaltecuhtli in two. Half of Tlaltecuhtli's body formed the sky, while the other half became the earth. Its shoulders became mountains, its hair plants and trees, and its eyes caves and wells. Despite the traditional depiction of this monster as female, some scholars have suggested that it was none other than Tlaloc. These scholars point to Tlaltecuhtli's goggling eyes as a link with caves and wells, and to his fanged mouth as a further connection with Tlaloc. Underpinning the theory is the idea that Tlaloc was an earth deity, as well as the god of rain and water. Translations of his name may well reinforce this view: while one meaning of *Tlaloc* is "He Who Makes Things Sprout," others include "One Who Lies on Earth" and "He Who is the Embodiment of the Earth."

Below: Carved from volcanic rock, this Aztec sculpture from the 13th century CE is an effigy either of Tlaloc himself or of a closely related Mesoamerican deity.

Worship of Tlaloc predated the Aztecs by many hundreds of years. Some scholars believe that the god was originally part of the pantheon of the Olmecs, the people who developed the first major civilization in Mesoamerica between about 1500 and 500 BCE. Evidence to support this view comes in the form of the abundance of Olmec statues and figurines with protruding mouths and jaguarlike teeth. Tlaloc was also an important god for Teotihuacanos, inhabitants of the powerful city of Teotihuacán that flourished between about 300 and 600 CE. One of the city's sacred monuments was a courtyard dedicated to Tlaloc. Several buildings were adorned with murals of the god's paradise, Tlalocan, depicting it as a place of lush plants and plentiful water; its inhabitants spent their time playing and relaxing. Teotihuacanos traded with another Mesoamerican people, the Maya (who flourished between about 200 and 900 CE), and both cultures seem to have influenced the other in a variety of ways. Tlaloc images have been discovered on carvings and inscriptions at Tikal, the Maya capital in present-day Guatemala.

Links with other deities

Tlaloc was linked to several other deities worshiped by Mesoamerican peoples, including Cocijo of the Zapotecs, Tzahui of the Mixtecs, and Tajin of the Totonac. In particular Chac, the Mayan rain god, possessed very similar characteristics to Tlaloc. Chac, too, had fanglike teeth and was sometimes worshiped not as a single deity but as four gods, the Chacs, who were associated with the four points of the compass. It is not hard to draw a parallel between these beings and the Tlaloques. In part, the connection between Tlaloc and other Mesoamerican deities was inevitable: all peoples in the region prayed to a rain god to secure good crops. However, the similarity of these rain gods cannot be explained by need alone—it suggests that Tlaloc was an ancient, pan-Mesoamerican deity.

ANDREW CAMPBELL

Bibliography

Arnold, Philip P. *Eating Landscape: Aztec and European Occupation of Tlalocan.* Niwot, CO: University of Colorado Press, 1999.

Ferguson, Diana. *Tales of the Plumed Serpent: Aztec, Inca and Maya Myths.* London: Collins and Brown, 2000.

Littleton, C. Scott, ed. *Mythology: The Illustrated Anthology of World Myth and Storytelling.* San Diego, CA: Thunder Bay Press, 2002.

Taube, Karl. *Aztec and Maya Myths.* London: British Museum Press, 1993.

SEE ALSO: Aztecs; Blood; Creation Myths; Fertility; Flood Myths; Maya; Natural Forces; Olmecs; Quetzalcoatl; Sacrifice.

TRITON

According to ancient Greek poet Hesiod (fl. 800 BCE), Triton was the son of Poseidon, god of the sea, and of Amphitrite, the sea queen. One myth claims that he lived with his parents in a golden palace at the bottom of the sea, and that he slept on a bed of sponges.

Triton was one of several minor Greek sea deities, including Nereus, Phorcys, Proteus, and Glaucus. Some of these sea gods assumed human form, but Triton was represented as a sea monster. He had a man's upper body and a head, which was usually bearded, and a long fish tail—occasionally this was divided into two flukes.

Triton is sometimes associated with centaurs, since in some Roman art he is represented with the forelegs of a horse. In Roman poetry Triton is well known for the hollow conch shell which he blows like a trumpet; the sound of his conch could drive back the waves, raise rocks and islands, and even frighten the giants when they were at war with the gods. In the *Aeneid* by Virgil (70–19 BCE), Triton was so proud of his musical talent that he became jealous of Misenus, the trumpeter of the Roman hero Aeneas. As Aeneas's ship approached the Bay of Naples, Triton drowned Misenus.

There are two versions of a traditional myth about Triton. According to one version, women from Tanagra in Boeotia came down to the sea for purification before the rites of Dionysus, god of wine. As they swam there, Triton disturbed them. They called to Dionysus for help, and he fought and defeated Triton. According to the other version,

Below: Swiss artist Arnold Böcklin (1827–1901) painted the sea god Triton aiding a Nereid. At right, a cupid appears in pursuit of the couple.

Right: Triton is represented drinking from his conch shell in this famous fountain in Rome, Italy, sculpted by Italian artist Gian Lorenzo Bernini (1598–1680).

Triton lay in ambush on the coast of Tanagra, waiting for cattle to be driven along the shore. He seized some of the animals as they passed; he also attacked small boats. The citizens of Tanagra placed a bowl of wine by the shore and Triton was attracted by the smell; he drank the wine and fell asleep by the sea. A man then came with an ax and cut off his head. Legend has it that in Hellenistic times the headless body of Triton was displayed at a temple in Tanagra.

In another myth Triton is associated with Libya and with a great Libyan lake that the Greeks called Lake Tritonis. Pindar (c. 522–c. 438 BCE) recounts that Jason and the Argonauts arrived there after a tidal wave swept their ship inland. Triton disguised himself as a local king called Euphemus and, welcoming the sailors, gave them a clod of earth as a gift. Greek historian Herodotus (c. 484–425 BCE) claimed that Triton received a golden tripod from the Argonauts, and that in return he showed them the way out of the lake to the sea. On the way to the sea, Triton took the clod of earth from the Argonauts and dropped it into the sea—it became the island of Thera. In this legend the magical creation of Thera may reflect how the Greeks colonized Libya: they used Thera as a stepping stone to reach the mainland. Herodotus mentions that on the island there was a sanctuary and an altar that were dedicated to Triton, but there remains little evidence of worship of Triton elsewhere. Scholars speculate that it is possible that Herodotus received his version from Greeks in Libya, who attributed qualities of a local deity to Triton.

Triton in art

In Etruscan, Hellenistic Greek, and Roman art and literature (and occasionally in earlier examples), Triton is often pluralized; a similar process happened with Cupid, Roman god of love, who was often transformed into a number of figures called cupids. In some forms of art, and especially in mosaics, tritons are depicted with Poseidon or other marine deities; and numerous tritons sometimes appear alongside cupids.

In Athenian art a frequent representation including Triton portrays an incident for which there is no literary source: a struggle between Triton and Heracles. Heracles had been charged to obtain the golden apples of the Hesperides for his 11th labor. He had to subdue the sea god Nereus so that he could learn the way to the garden of the Hesperides, where the golden apples grew. Heracles' struggle with Nereus is represented a number of times in early art. From the mid-sixth century BCE onward, however, Nereus was replaced by Triton. In some examples, Nereus appears as a third character in the scene—as a witness to the battle. Some scholars suggest that cultural changes brought about by migration or invasion could have been responsible for introducing new deities, or replacing older gods and goddesses. It is uncertain why Athenian artists substituted Triton for Nereus, however.

For Romans, tritons became a frequent pictorial motif in mosaics, cameos, sculptured reliefs, terra-cottas, bronzes, and most other media. Some representations of tritons were female. In Etruscan art tritons were sometimes depicted as male and female members of couples.

Although Triton is rarely mentioned in mythology, he was always considered to be a personification of the waves and the power of the ocean.

JAMES M. REDFIELD

Bibliography
Hesiod, and M. L. West, trans. *Theogony; and Works and Days.* New York: Oxford University Press, 1999.
Virgil, and Robert Fitzgerald, trans. *The Aeneid.* New York: Vintage, 1990.

SEE ALSO: Eros; Heracles; Nymphs; Poseidon; Sea.

TROILUS

The role of the Trojan prince Troilus in the Trojan War varied according to different authors. In some accounts he was a great warrior, in others a defenseless boy. All versions agree, however, that Troilus was killed by the Greek hero Achilles—it was prophesied that Troy would never fall if the youth reached the age of 20.

According to most sources Troilus was the son of Priam and Hecuba, king and queen of Troy. In a version provided by Greek dramatist Apollodorus (third century BCE), however, the youth's father was Apollo, god of light and prophecy. Some authors regarded Troilus as a relatively unimportant character in the Trojan War: Greek poet Homer (c. ninth–eighth century BCE), for instance, referred only to his death in the epic the *Iliad*—perhaps because Homer felt that Troilus was too young to take part in the fighting. However, much later works, such as those believed to be by Dictys of Crete and Dares the Phrygian, which were translated into Latin around the fourth and fifth centuries CE, respectively, portray Troilus as one of the great heroes of Troy. According to the work by Dares, Troilus was a large and handsome boy who was strong for his age, brave, and eager for glory. He was a fierce fighter who wreaked havoc among the Greeks, especially after the death of his brother Hector at the hands of Achilles. In this version of events, the Greek warriors Diomedes and Odysseus both considered Troilus to be the bravest of men and the equal of Hector.

The death of Troilus
Most accounts agree on the manner of Troilus's death: he was ambushed outside the city of Troy by Achilles, who killed him with his spear in a sanctuary of Apollo. There are, however, differences in the details of Troilus's death. The best-known version comes not from a text but from a vase painting. The sixth-century-BCE François Krater (a vessel used for diluting wine with water) depicts a variety of scenes connected with the murder. In one, Achilles hides while Troilus, on horseback, accompanies his sister Polyxena as she draws water from a fountain. In another, Achilles runs after Troilus, who attempts to flee on his horse. In yet another scene Achilles, who has captured the youth, kills him on Apollo's altar. In the epic *Aeneid* by Roman poet Virgil (70–19 BCE), Troilus flees from Achilles in a chariot, only to become entangled in his horses' reins.

Troilus and Criseyde: a medieval romance
The story with which Troilus is most famously associated comes not from the Graeco-Roman era but the medieval one. The biggest influence on this story was the Latin translations of Dictys and Dares. Until the Renaissance in the 15th and 16th centuries CE, the art of reading ancient Greek was largely lost in the Western world. Consequently the most important sources of Greek mythology—such as Homer's epics—were not available to medieval authors, who had to rely on existing Latin versions of the story of the Trojan War. Although scholars argue that the literary value of the works by Dictys and Dares is limited, it is thought that they constituted an important source of information and inspiration for the medieval romances involving Troilus.

English poet Geoffrey Chaucer's (c. 1342–1400) *Troilus and Criseyde* begins with the narrator sketching the background. Calchas, a Trojan priest, foresees that Troy will fall and therefore defects to the Greek camp, leaving his daughter Criseyde behind in the city. Troilus, a handsome and valiant Trojan prince, falls in love with Criseyde but has no idea how to pursue her. Meanwhile Criseyde, as a young widow, is concerned to maintain her chaste reputation. With the help of Criseyde's uncle Pandarus, who is a good friend of Troilus and more than happy to act as a go-between, Troilus manages to visit Criseyde and win her heart. Their happiness, however, is short-lived: the Trojans lose a battle, and one of their elders, Antenor, is captured. In the Greek camp, Calchas reminds the Greeks that Troy will soon fall and asks them to ensure that his daughter will be reunited with him. The Greeks agree to trade Antenor for Criseyde. In the city, the news

Above: This fresco (c. 550–c. 520 BCE) depicts Troilus on horseback. The fresco comes from the Tomb of the Bulls in Tarquinia, Italy.

comes as a devastating blow to the lovers, who are forced to remain silent about their affair: to reveal it would destroy Criseyde's reputation. The exchange takes place and the pair separate, but only after Criseyde has promised that she will return within 10 days. Soon, however, Criseyde's love for Troilus proves untrue. She accepts the advances of her Greek escort, Diomedes, and betrays Troilus for fear of being left without a protector. Not long afterward, Troilus is killed in battle. Chaucer, however, refuses to put all the blame on Criseyde, whom he considers equally with Troilus to be a victim of love and fortune: "I cannot find it in my heart to chide this hapless woman more than the story will; her name, alas, is punished far and wide, and that should be sufficient for the ill she did; I would excuse her for it still."

Different Versions of Troilus and Criseyde

Chaucer's *Troilus and Criseyde* was one of several versions of the story in the medieval period and later. Chaucer's lengthy poem, composed around 1385, was an adaptation of the work by Italian poet Giovanni Boccaccio (1313–1375), *Il filostrato* (The Love Struck). In turn, Boccaccio's poem was influenced by the 12th-century French poem *Roman de Troie* by Benoît de Sainte-Maure. This poem, which contains the earliest known version of the Troilus and Criseyde story, was a reworking of Homer's *Iliad* based on the works attributed to Dares the Phrygian and Dictys of Crete; it was also heavily influenced by the medieval society in which Benoît de Sainte-Maure lived.

In the late 15th century, at the end of the medieval period, Scottish poet Robert Henryson (c. 1425– c. 1508) took up the theme of the two lovers in *The Testament of Cresseid*, which forms a continuation of Chaucer's story. In Henryson's poem, after Cresseid (Criseyde) betrays Troilus, she is punished by the gods with leprosy. When Troilus finally meets her again he fails to recognize her in her diseased state. Shakespeare (1564–1616) also wrote a version of the story, *Troilus and Cressida*. While some scholars have compared this play unfavorably to his other works, others argue that it should be regarded as a clever alternative to, rather than a flawed example of, a classical tragedy.

Left: A 19th-century engraving depicting Cressida from Shakespeare's Troilus and Cressida. *The medieval character Cressida, or Criseyde, was based on the classical figure of Chryseis, who was captured by the Greeks. The revenge of her father, Chryses, had severe repercussions for the Greeks.*

The love story of Troilus and Criseyde was a medieval invention. While the accounts by Chaucer and other writers (see box, above) were presented as an ancient tale, with characters' names taken from the legend of Troy, the passions of those characters and their interrelationships were very different from the Greek versions. For example, Criseyde can be identified as Chryseis, the daughter of the Trojan priest Chryses, but in the medieval story her father was a much more famous priest named Calchas. The fact that Calchas was actually a Greek priest seems not to have bothered the medieval audience—if they were even aware of such discrepancies. The Trojan War served merely as a setting for a typical medieval story in which everything revolved around the courtly love of the main characters. Although the Trojan heroes were valiant in battle, they put their romantic interests ahead of their exploits on the battlefield, and love became the main focus of the story.

FEYO SCHUDDEBOOM

Bibliography

Apollodorus, and Robin Hard, trans. *The Library of Greek Mythology*. New York: Oxford University Press, 1999.

Chaucer, and Nevill Coghill, trans. *Troilus and Criseyde*. London: Penguin, 1971.

Hamilton, Edith. *Mythology*. Boston, MA: Black Bay Books, 1998.

Homer, and Robert Fagles, trans. *The Iliad*. New York: Penguin USA, 2003.

SEE ALSO: Achilles; Apollo; Hector; Hecuba; Priam.

TYCHE

Tyche was the Greek goddess of chance and was known as Fortuna by the Romans. According to Greek poet Hesiod (fl. 800 BCE), Tyche was the daughter of the Titans Oceanus and Tethys, although other writers claimed that Zeus (king of the gods) was her father.

The ocean has always been notoriously unpredictable, and its mythological inhabitants shared in its fickle nature. Tyche, whose name can be translated as "chance," "fortune," "fate," "success," "destiny," or "luck," belonged to a small group of deities such as Eros (god of love) whose names described their functions. While Tyche was recognized as a goddess fairly early, her personality did not develop until quite late, during the Hellenistic period (323–30 BCE). At that time cities and officials adopted Tyche as their patron deity, and people made dedications and sacrifices at her shrines.

Tyche was associated primarily with good luck. She was depicted as a female wearing a turreted crown and carrying a horn of plenty in one hand and a ship's rudder in the other. The crown of city walls symbolized the fact that she directed cities' destinies, the horn represented the prosperity she brought, and the rudder symbolized fortune. Tyche's rise in popularity after the classical period (in Athens this was about 479–338 BCE) signified the extent to which the Greeks believed that chance governed their lives.

Above: Archaeologists date the construction of this colossal stone head of Tyche to c. 50 BCE. It stands on the slope of Mount Nimrod in Turkey.

The role of fate in the Greek world

Like most people, the Greeks desired to understand their world, both to control it and to render it less arbitrary and frightening. The Olympian gods were the earliest systematic attempt to account for everyday events.

Tyche was the default explanation for anything that was not attributable to these deities. It was no contradiction for *Tyche* to mean both "chance" and "fate." In Greek thought, fate was unstoppable. Fortune was the revelation of that fate, and destiny was the fulfillment of that fortune. When fortune was beneficial, it was called luck or success, and when not, it was chance.

Tyche in literature

While early writers sometimes personified Tyche as a goddess, most of the time they referred to an impersonal *tyche*. One of the earliest mentions of Tyche was in the 12th Olympian ode of Greek poet Pindar (c. 522–c. 438 BCE), which celebrated an athletic victory. In the poem

Left: Tyche is depicted with the horn of plenty, a symbol of prosperity, in this sixth-century-CE mosaic in Jordan.

catastrophe. She was often addressed euphemistically, as if by naming her "kindly" or "savior" she might be persuaded to bring good luck instead of bad.

Greek comic dramatist Menander (c. 342–c. 292 BCE) called Tyche a blind goddess, although this description may have referred more to her indiscriminate ways than to her physicality. Tyche delivers the prologue in Menander's play *The Shield*, announcing that she plans a surprise ending.

Hellenistic historian Polybius (c. 200–c. 118 BCE) used Tyche to explain otherwise inexplicable historical events. Tyche also presided over human affairs in Greek novels, which date from the Roman period (after 30 BCE). In these, Tyche personified the chaotic world: pirate raids, slavery, shipwrecks, mistaken identities, and chance occurrences. The novels are equally ambivalent about how to cope with Tyche. In some, another god overrides her mischief; others reduce her to the expression "by chance." Tyche represented the unknown, and people alternately appeased and disparaged her as human hopes rose and fell.

Philosophical approaches to Tyche

Greek philosopher Plato (c. 428–c. 348 BCE) identified Tyche as the spontaneous cause of divine actions, and his pupil Aristotle (384–322 BCE) conceived of her impersonally as spontaneity itself. The philosophical schools that grew out of Platonic and Aristotelian thought, notably Stoicism and Epicureanism, dealt particularly with the problem of chance. The Stoics defined Tyche as "a cause unclear to human understanding," suggesting that her workings would be logical to a higher intelligence. The Epicureans adopted a mechanistic view of the universe— in their view there was no such thing as chance, and even seemingly random occurrences could be explained by the movement of matter.

There were three famous ancient Greek statues of Tyche, now lost—two by Praxiteles (370–330 BCE) and one by Eutychides (third century BCE).

KATHERYN CHEW

Bibliography
Bulfinch, Thomas. *Bulfinch's Mythology.* New York: Modern Library, 1998.
Howatson, M. C., and Ian Chilvers. *Concise Oxford Companion to Classical Literature.* New York: Oxford University Press, 1993.

Pindar called Tyche the daughter of Zeus, unlike Hesiod's genealogy, which made Tyche and Zeus cousins. Perhaps Pindar wished to imply that Zeus had some sway over Tyche, and that the universe was under his control and was not subject to the whims of chance.

Tyche was entirely absent from the epics of Greek poet Homer (c. ninth–eighth century BCE), simply because there was no need for a goddess of chance in Homer's world—everything in his stories developed under the careful providence of other deities.

In the Greek dramas, Tyche occasionally engineered unexpected outcomes—an unforeseen reprieve or a sudden

SEE ALSO: Nymphs; Oceanus; Zeus.

TYPHON

In Greek mythology Typhon was a hideous monster with a hundred dragons' heads. He was best known as the personification of volcanic forces.

Typhon was the youngest son of Gaia (Earth) and Tartarus (the underworld). Fire shone forth from his eyes, red-hot lava poured from his gaping mouths, and he made every kind of noise—sometimes he spoke articulately like a human, but at others he bellowed like a bull, roared like a lion, barked like a dog, or hissed like a snake. Whatever his form of utterance, his voice made the mountains echo. Typhon terrorized the universe, and he would have conquered it if Zeus had not intervened and struck him with a thunderbolt. There followed a long battle between them during which the sea boiled and the mountains melted like metals in a foundry. At length Zeus cast Typhon down into Tartarus. In this way the eternal rule of Zeus over the universe was finally established. In some versions of the myth, Typhon was confined after his defeat either in the land of the Arimi in Cilicia (the eastern Mediterranean coastal region of Asia Minor, part of modern Turkey), under Mount Etna in Sicily, or in other volcanic regions, where he was the cause of eruptions. Typhon was thus the personification of volcanic forces. Among Typhon's children by his wife, Echidna, were Cerberus, the three-headed hound of hell; the multiheaded Hydra of Lerna; the Chimaera; and the Sphinx. Typhon was also father of dangerous winds (typhoons), and he was identified by later writers with Egyptian god Seth.

Embellished accounts

The earliest description of Typhon (or Typhoes) occurs in the *Theogony* by Greek poet Hesiod (fl. 800 BCE). Nearly seven centuries later Apollodorus (fl. 140 BCE) tells

essentially the same story with additional details. Typhon, he says, was the largest child of Gaia. From the thighs upward he had the form of a man, but he was taller than mountains and his head sometimes touched the stars. From the thighs downward he had the shape of two enormous vipers. He also had wings and tangled hair that streamed from his head and chin. When Typhon began to throw rocks at heaven, the gods fled to Egypt and turned themselves into animals. (This is probably intended to explain the animal form of Egyptian deities.) Zeus attacked Typhon with a sickle, but Typhon wrested the weapon from his grip and used it to cut out the tendons of Zeus's hands and feet. He then dragged Zeus off and imprisoned him inside a cave. Hermes and Pan together recovered the tendons and healed Zeus, who this time came after Typhon in a chariot drawn by winged horses. The Fates tricked Typhon by

Below: The painting encircling this Greek vase from the seventh or sixth century BCE depicts Typhon. Both sides of the vase are shown.

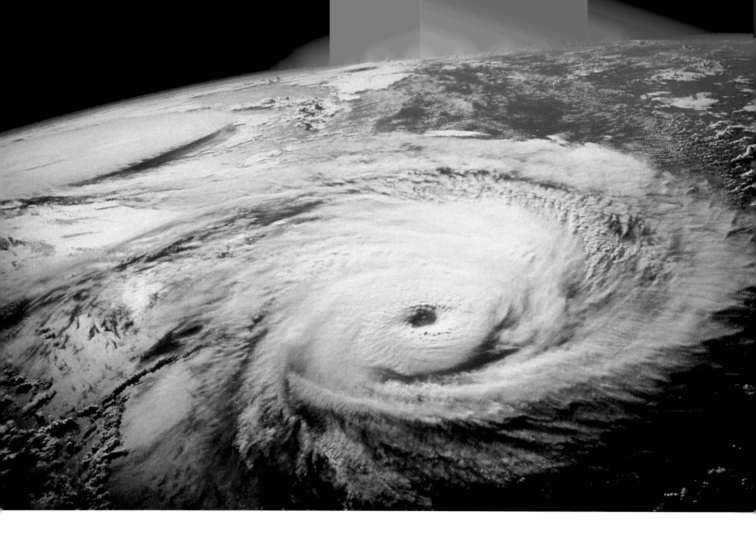

Above: A typhoon photographed from space. The name Typhon *comes from Greek* typhon, *meaning "violent whirlwind."*

offering him food that they told him would make him invulnerable but which in fact weakened him. Zeus then took his chance and drove Typhon across the sea to Sicily. There Zeus piled Mount Etna on top of the monster; the smoke and fire emitted by the volcano were thought to be the thunderbolts with which Zeus subdued him. Thus Typhon lives on—he was never destroyed, merely subjugated. He remains a force of chaos and destruction, and may be held in check only for as long as Zeus's peace is preserved—the price of order is eternal vigilance. Of the many other authors who have written about the Typhon legend, the most famous are Greek playwright Aeschylus (525–456 BCE) and Roman poet Ovid (43 BCE–17 CE).

Typhon and the struggle between Zeus and Hera

Another version of the story, dating from at least the sixth century BCE, makes the birth of Typhon an episode in the endless marital strife between Zeus and his consort Hera. When Zeus gave birth to goddess Athena on his own, Hera was angry. She wanted to prove that she could do anything

Zeus could do, so she alone produced Typhon, and his brother Hephaestus. Since Athena had no father, and Typhon had no mother, they were antithetical figures—always opposed to each other. In one early Greek myth Athena showed her courage above all other gods by single-handedly defending Mount Olympus when it was attacked by Typhon. All the other gods fled in terror, but Athena battled with the monster while at the same time goading her father, Zeus, into action. Eventually Zeus plucked up his courage and returned to the fray, striking the monster with his thunderbolts. In this account it was Athena, not Zeus, who threw Mount Etna on top of Typhon, crushing the monster underneath.

JAMES M. REDFIELD

Bibliography

Bulfinch, Thomas. *Bulfinch's Mythology.* New York: Modern Library, 1998.

Hesiod, and M. L. West, trans. *Theogony; and Works and Days.* New York: Oxford University Press, 1999.

Ovid, and A. D. Melville, trans. *Metamorphoses.* New York: Oxford University Press, 1998.

SEE ALSO: Athena; Gaia; Heracles; Hermes; Natural Forces; Pan; Seth; Zeus.

URANUS

For the ancient Greeks, Uranus, the personification of the sky, was the first ruler of the universe. He was the father and grandfather of many of the most important gods in the Greek pantheon.

According to the Greek creation myth, elucidated by the poet Hesiod (fl. 800 BCE), Uranus was predated by four beings: Chaos (the void), Gaia (the earth), Tartarus (the region far below the earth), and Eros (sexual love). From Chaos came the basic cyclical divisions of time, Erebus (Darkness), Nyx (Night), Aether (Brightness), and Hemera (Day); but it was Gaia who created the primary physical divisions of the world: Pontus (the oceans), Ourea (the mountains), and Uranus (the sky).

Father and grandfather of a pantheon

Once he was brought into being, Uranus became the first all-powerful ruler in the universe and the ultimate procreator. He lifted himself up into the sky by day, but at night came back down to lie on Gaia, his mother. Their union resulted in a number of children, from whom were descended all the generations of gods and other creatures who wielded power in the universe. Uranus and Gaia were the parents of the 12 Titans: Oceanus, Coeus, Crius, Hyperion, Iapetus, Theia, Rhea, Themis, Mnemosyne, Phoebe, Tethys, and Cronus. In addition, they produced the three gigantic, one-eyed Cyclopes—Brontes, Steropes, and Arges—and the three Hecatoncheires (Hundred-Handed Ones)—Briareos, Cottus, and Gyges. Each of the latter had a hundred arms and 50 heads.

Below: The Mutilation of Uranus *by Italian artist Giorgio Vasari (1511–1574). Vasari's painting shows Uranus's son Cronus wielding the sickle that he used to sever his father's genitals.*

Left: A spectrograph of Uranus provides an enhanced impression of the planet's blue-green color that associates it with the sky.

A heavenly host

Many of Uranus's descendants reflected his association with the heavens. The children of the Titan Hyperion and the Titaness Theia were Helios (Sun), Selene (Moon), and Eos (Dawn), while Hyperion himself was also sometimes identified as the sun. Another Titan, Astraeus, was closely connected with the sky at both day and night—Astraeus's name means "Starry," and his children were the North, South, East, and West Winds, as well as all the stars. The Titan Coeus and the Titaness Phoebe had a daughter, Leto, and, through her, two grandchildren, the Olympian deities Artemis and Apollo. Artemis had a close association with the moon, and was sometimes identified with Selene, while her brother was linked to the sun in his guise as Phoebus Apollo (the Shining One). Even Uranus's monstrous offspring the Cyclopes had heavenly associations, revealed by their names: Brontes ("Thunderer"), Steropes ("Lightner") and Arges ("Flashing").

Furthermore, despite Uranus's role as a primal figure, associated with a stage in the creation of the universe that was full of elemental and crude beings, he was the father of a number of divinities who represented order and creativity. Through his daughter Mnemosyne (Memory) he was the grandfather of the nine Muses, who inspired every form of creativity. His granddaughter Urania was the Muse of astronomy. Through the Titaness Themis he was the grandfather of some of the most powerful principles of regularity in the world: the three Horae (Seasons) and the three Moirai (Fates).

As in many other cosmologies from the Mediterranean and western Asia, therefore, the first generative pair in the Greek account of creation were Earth and Sky. The nature of Uranus's coupling with Gaia supports the suggestion that the deity's name is connected to the ancient Greek word for dew: Uranus descended on Earth, bringing the sky's moisture—dew, mist, and rain—that fertilized the ground.

Naming the Planets

Modern astronomers have drawn heavily on Greek mythology to find appropriate names for the planets and other important bodies in the solar system, and Uranus—the third-largest planet in the solar system—is no exception. Uranus, which was discovered in 1781, is the seventh planet in order of distance from the sun. Appropriately for a planet named for the Greek personification of the sky, Uranus appears blue-green, the result of the absorption of red light by methane gas in its atmosphere.

In 2004 a group of astronomers believed that they had discovered a 10th planet, located around 8 billion miles (13 billion km) from Earth. However, other scientists argued that, at a mere 1,100 miles (1,800 km) in diameter, the discovery only merited the term *planetoid*. The name astronomers gave to their sighting continued a broadening of tradition to include nonclassical mythology. This name was Sedna, for the Inuit sea goddess. In myth, Sedna's wild temper and voracious appetite led her parents to take her out to sea in a boat and cast her overboard. So desperate was Sedna to hold on to the boat that her father was forced to sever her fingers, one by one, to make her let go. She then sank to the bottom of the ocean, which became her domain. The cold world Sedna inhabited made her name an appropriate choice for the planet orbiting in the farthest icy reaches of the solar system.

Sons against fathers

Uranus, however, had no love for his children. On the contrary, he was a forceful, autocratic figure who was unwilling to contemplate any challenge to his position and so hated his offspring. He refused to allow his children even to be born and instead held them back inside Gaia. She was unable to bear the pain caused by this act of suppression and decided to take action against her partner. She created a sickle out of adamant and urged her children to use it in rebellion against their father. All of them were too afraid to do so—with the sole exception of Gaia's youngest son, Cronus, who agreed to lie in ambush one night and attack his father.

As day turned into night, Uranus returned as usual to settle on Gaia. He was set upon by Cronus, who, reaching out with his left hand and wielding Gaia's sickle in his right, cut off his father's genitals and flung them into the sea. By this act of violence Uranus was deposed by Cronus, who released all his brothers and sisters from Gaia's womb. Consequently, the Titans replaced their parents as the dominant generation of gods. However, Cronus took after his father, both in the tyranny of his rule and in his fear of being overthrown by the children his wife Rhea bore him—a fear that led him to swallow each child after its birth. In the end, however, Cronus was deposed by his children, just as Uranus had been. Uranus himself was only too happy to participate in the downfall of his rebellious son. He advised his daughter Rhea on strategies to ensure that her son Zeus survived to adulthood and to make Cronus release the children he had swallowed, thus providing Zeus with much-needed allies.

While the castration of Uranus signified the end of his reign, it also resulted in the creation of several new divinities. From the combination of Uranus's genitals and the elemental waters of the sea into which they were thrown came the beautiful love goddess Aphrodite. Drops of blood from Uranus's castration that fell on Gaia also led her to produce three other sets of beings. The first were the three Furies—Alecto, Megaera, and Tisiphone—whose role, appropriately in view of their origin, was to exact vengeance on crimes of violence committed within families. Second were the Giants, huge and hideous creatures who mounted an unsuccessful rebellion against the Olympian gods, a battle known as the Gigantomachy. Third and finally, the mingling of Uranus's blood with Gaia produced the Meliads, the nymphs of ash trees. In addition, according to one tradition, the sickle that Cronus threw away after the attack on his father fell to the earth, where it formed the Greek island of Corcyra (modern Corfu).

Rivalry and violence

The graphic violence that features in the story of Uranus's overthrow by Cronus seems to have shocked some of the ancient Greeks themselves. The philosopher Plato (c. 428–c. 348 BCE), for instance, suggested that the account should be censored and withheld almost entirely from the young. However, the central motif of violence and castration is not uniquely Greek. In Anatolia (part of modern Turkey), the creation myth that the Hittites adopted

Left: An 18th-century engraving of Cronus by Italian artist Giovanni Cavattoni. Gaia's sickle is depicted at the Titan's feet.

Left: Mnemosyne *by English artist Dante Gabriel Rossetti (1828–1882). Mnemosyne was one of the many offspring of Uranus and Gaia. She was the mother of the nine Muses.*

from the Hurrian people told how the father god Kumarbi attacked his master, the creator god Anu, by biting off Anu's testicles. Anu's seed grew inside Kumarbi until he gave birth to three children, including the weather god Teshub, who overthrew his father. The underlying pattern of events of the Greek and Hittite myths is strikingly similar, and some scholars believe that some kind of common ancestry may well link the two accounts.

Separating Earth from Sky

Greek mythology, like that of many other ancient cultures, regarded the earth and the sky as the two primary sources for the rest of creation, and the separation of this pair was a critical step in the cosmogony of the world. Some scholars believe that the separation occurred with Gaia's creation of Uranus, an act of parthenogenesis (self-reproduction) that created Sky as an entity distinct from Earth. Other scholars argue that it was Cronus who caused the division between the heavens and the earth when he castrated his father—so preventing Uranus from lying on Gaia and fertilizing her.

The separation of the earth and sky finds a strong parallel in Egyptian mythology. The Egyptians believed that their sky deity, Nut, was female; in contrast, Geb (Earth)

Above: The southern coastline of the Greek island of Corfu. According to myth, Corfu was formed when Cronus discarded the sickle that he had used to castrate Uranus, and it fell to the earth.

was male. Nut married Geb and bore him four children. In one version of the story, however, the deities' father, Shu, god of air, had to separate the couple because they were holding on to one another so tightly that none of their children could emerge. Once the sky was pried away from the earth, over which it formed an arch, the next generation of gods could come forth. However, unlike his Greek counterpart, the Egyptian earth deity grieved after his parting from the sky. The Egyptians believed that Geb's distress at the loss of Nut was the cause of earthquakes.

Uranus in Roman myth

Roman mythology gives a much less prominent role to the process of cosmogony and the early stages of the creation of the universe, but it does attribute a similar role to Uranus, who is identified as a sky god, born of elemental parentage early in the history of the universe. Unlike the Greek account, however, the Roman Uranus does not emerge from an act of parthenogenesis and instead has two parents, the Titans Oceanus and Tethys. These parents themselves represent a major difference from the Greek version made famous by Hesiod, who counted Oceanus and Tethys among the offspring of Uranus and Gaia.

Another difference between the accounts is that, according to Roman beliefs, Uranus was the brother of the earth goddess Tellus. In the Roman story, Uranus and Tellus were the earliest divine couple, who gave birth to the gods Jupiter (the equivalent of the Greek Zeus), Vulcan (the Greek god was Hephaestus), and Venus (the Greek goddess was Aphrodite) without an intermediate generation.

In Roman relief sculpture and sarcophagi, Uranus sometimes appeared representing the firmament of heaven, often paired with Tellus in scenes representing the glory of the Roman Empire. The deity was also depicted in specific myths, such as in the Judgment of Paris, the creation of man by Prometheus, and the fall of Helios's son Phaethon.

ANTHONY BULLOCH

Bibliography
Hesiod, and M. L. West, trans. *Theogony; and Works and Days.* New York: Oxford University Press, 1999.

March, Jenny. *Cassell's Dictionary of Classical Mythology.* London: Cassell, 1998.

Storm, Rachel. *The Encyclopaedia of Eastern Mythology.* London: Lorenz Books, 1999.

Turcan, Robert, and Antonia Nevill, trans. *The Gods of Ancient Rome: Religion in Everyday Life from Archaic to Imperial Times.* New York: Routledge, 2001.

SEE ALSO: Aphrodite; Apollo; Creation Myths; Cronus; Cyclopes; Fates; Furies; Gaia; Giants; Hittites; Muses; Nut; Nyx; Oedipus; Phaethon; Sky; Titans; Zeus.

VALKYRIES

Valkyries, meaning "Choosers of the Slain," were beautiful young women—sometimes immortal, depending on the Norse myth—who scouted battlefields looking for the bravest of slain warriors. Once they found the chosen warriors, they would escort them to Valhalla, hall of the chief god, Odin. There the Valkyries waited on the warriors, who prepared themselves for Ragnarok.

In ancient Norse mythology, before they were linked to Odin and Ragnarok, the Valkyries were thought of as corpse goddesses and were sometimes represented in carvings as carrion-eating ravens. The original Valkyries, appearing on battlefields as soon as the fighting was over, would weave tapestries from the intestines of slain warriors and feed corpses to their pet wolves.

Between the 3rd and 11th centuries, the perception of the Valkyries changed and they became associated with Odin, ruler of the gods. Mortal maidens or princesses could become Valkyries, and they were described as beautiful young women armed with helmets and spears who rode winged horses onto battlefields. Freya, Norse goddess of love and beauty, was often depicted as a Valkyrie, armed with a corselet (armor covering one's trunk), helmet, shield, and spear. The Valkyries were sometimes called swan maidens, and in some myths they were clothed in swan feathers that enabled them to fly.

On the battlefield the Valkyries chose the souls of the bravest slain warriors to become Einherjar, soldiers to fight for Odin at Ragnarok, the final battle between the gods and the giants. The Valkyries escorted the new Einherjar across Bifröst, the rainbow bridge that linked Midgard (world of mortals) to Asgard (world of the gods), and on into Valhalla. Once inside Valhalla, the Valkyries changed clothes. Wearing simple white robes, they served the Einherjar fine foods, such as wild boar, and sacred wine made from honey. They would remain the Einherjar's servants until Ragnarok.

Messengers of Odin

The Valkyries were also Odin's bodyguards and messengers. Whenever the chief god sent them out, mortals saw their flickering armor and light streaming from their spears. In the Middle Ages (c. 500–c. 1500 CE), Scandinavians believed the northern lights (aurora borealis) were the Valkyries flying across the night sky. They also believed that life-giving dew fell from the manes of the Valkyries' horses.

Left: The Rhinemaidens *by German painter Hermann Hendrich (1854–1931). As rightful owners of Sigurd's magic ring, these water nymphs played an important role in the story of the Valkyrie Brynhild and Sigurd, her lover.*

Right: Brynhild was a popular Valkyrie in Norse mythology. Arthur Rackham (1867–1939) depicted her in his 20th-century illustration.

Although the Valkyries were most often depicted as battle maidens, they were not warriors. The medieval perception of the battle-dressed Valkyries may have come from the contemporary discovery of prehistoric burial sites of ancient female warriors interred with their weapons.

In Danish folklore it was said that the Valkyries were able to predict the outcome of a battle by unfurling a flag called the Raven Banner. The banner was woven by the Valkyries from pure white silk and normally had no image or design. When it was unveiled during a battle, however, a raven would magically appear in the center, prophesying the battle's outcome. If the raven's beak was wide open and its wings flapped, then the Danes would be victorious. If the raven remained motionless, the Danes would lose.

Valkyries usually appeared in groups of nine. Grouping varied depending on the version or source, but common groups included Brynhild, Goll, Gondul, Herfjotur, Hlokk, Hrist, Mist, Reginleif, Sigrdrifa, Sigrun, Skeggjold, Skogul, and Svava. Many were named in the Icelandic *Prose Edda* and *Poetic Edda* (see box, page 1403). They were also either featured or mentioned in the German *Nibelungenlied* ("Song of the Nibelungs"), the Norse *Völsunga Saga*, and the Norwegian *Thiorekssaga* ("Deeds of Thioreks").

The *Völsunga Saga* gives perhaps the most famous story of a Valkyrie, Brynhild, of her love for the hero Sigurd, and of the conniving interference of Gudrún, a princess. The long and complicated myth is an example of what happens, in Brynhild's case, when Odin is disobeyed and, for Sigurd, when a Valkyrie is spurned.

Brynhild defied Odin when she let the wrong king die in a battle. As punishment, Odin condemned her to marry a mortal, but she swore she would marry only the bravest.

Morrigan: A Celtic Valkyrie

In Celtic mythology there was a battle goddess named Morrigan who shared many characteristics with the Valkyries. For example, both Morrigan and the Valkyries were believed to be able to predict a warrior's death in battle, and they were closely associated with ravens. Morrigan was one of the Tuatha Dé Danaan, meaning "people of the goddess Danu." The Tuatha Dé Danaan were, according to legend, one of the five mythic races who invaded and inhabited ancient Ireland. At the First Battle of Mag Tuireadh, Morrigan was instrumental in defeating the Firbolg, the mythic peoples who preceded the Tuatha Dé Danaan. At the Second Battle of Mag Tuireadh, she helped the Tuatha Dé Danaan to victory over the Fomorians, a race of giants.

Morrigan also appeared to the hero Cú Chulainn. She offered him her love, but he rejected her. Later, she warned him that she would hinder him in battle by settling on his shoulder disguised as a raven. Then, when he was marching to his final battle, he again met the battle goddess, who had transformed herself into a washerwoman. She told him that she was washing the clothes and armor of the dead hero, Cú Chulainn.

From then on Brynhild slept within a ring of fire on the mountaintop called Hindafjall, where she waited for the bravest hero to ride through the flames to be at her side. Sigurd was the only warrior courageous and skilled enough to breach the flames. The pair quickly fell in love. In time, however, Sigurd had to leave, vowing to return. As he departed, he gave Brynhild a magic ring as a token of his love. The ring was part of the bounty he had captured from a dragon's lair before he had met Brynhild. When Sigurd left, Brynhild slept again within the ring of fire and waited for her lover to return.

Gudrún tricks Sigurd

When Sigurd reached the kingdom of Gjúkung (known as Nibelung in German mythology), he swore a brotherhood oath with its ruler, King Gjúki. Gudrún, the beautiful daughter of Gjúki, and sister of Gunnar, fell in love with Sigurd as soon as she saw him, but Sigurd refused her advances because of his devotion to Brynhild. Gudrún, however, had dreamed that she was destined to be Sigurd's lover and that after Sigurd's death she would marry Brynhild's brother, Atli. Her dream also prophesied that Atli would kill her own brothers. To make Sigurd forget Brynhild, Gudrún's mother, the witch Grímhild, secretly slipped a magic potion into his drink. Soon after drinking it, Sigurd fell in love with Gudrún.

Meanwhile, Gunnar decided to marry the abandoned Brynhild, but he could not ride through the ring of fire to reach her. Grímhild concocted another magic potion, this time to make Sigurd look like Gunnar. Once the potion took effect, Sigurd, in the guise of Gunnar, rode through the flames and convinced Brynhild to accept that her lover was not going to return and that she should marry him (Gunnar). Saddened but not wanting to be alone, Brynhild agreed. Before they left Hindafjall, Brynhild gave her new fiancé Sigurd's magic ring in exchange for one of Gunnar's.

Three days later the pair reached Gjúkung. Without Brynhild knowing, Sigurd turned back into his true self, and the real Gunnar married Brynhild. Soon afterward, the magic of the first potion, which had made Sigurd forget his love for Brynhild, wore off. It was too late, however; Brynhild was married to Gunnar and he to Gudrún.

Brynhild's revenge

Several years later Gudrún and Brynhild argued over whose husband was better. Brynhild said that Gunnar was the best because he had ridden through the flames for her. Gudrún revealed how it had been not Gunnar but Sigurd disguised as Gunnar. She then showed Brynhild Sigurd's magic ring to prove her story. Brynhild had never stopped loving Sigurd, but she was blind with rage.

To have her revenge, Brynhild falsely accused Sigurd of raping her when they had traveled from Hindafjall, thus dishonoring his oath of brotherhood with Gunnar. She threatened to leave Gunnar if he did not kill Sigurd. Because of the oath, however, Gunnar could not kill Sigurd himself. Instead he got his brother Gutthorm to do it.

When eventually the two warriors faced each other, Gutthorm fatally stabbed Sigurd, but Sigurd was able to kill Gutthorm by spearing him in the back. As he lay dying, Sigurd was held by Gudrún, while Brynhild laughed insanely with both grief and rage. At Sigurd's funeral, Brynhild gleefully told Gunnar that Sigurd had not raped her, and that as a Valkyrie she predicted the violent deaths of all Gudrún's children, even the ones not yet born. Brynhild then threw herself onto Sigurd's funeral pyre and perished.

Years later, Atli, Brynhild's brother, and Gudrún married and had two sons, Erpr and Eitill. Realizing that Atli had married her only to gain the treasure that Sigurd had taken from the dragon's lair and to avenge Brynhild's death, Gudrún sent the

Left: This sixth-century-CE silver pendant from Sweden represents a Valkyrie offering a horn. Archaeologists suggest that the horn is for holding a drink, indicating the Valkyries' role as servants of the Einherjar.

magic ring to her brothers as a warning to guard the treasure and that their lives were in danger. The brothers hid Sigurd's treasure in the Rhine, but could not avoid Atli. He killed them all. When she learned of her brothers' deaths, Gudrún, like Medea of Greek mythology, killed her sons Erpr and Eitill, roasted their hearts, and served them to Atli when he was drunk. Then she killed him too.

Gudrún later married King Jónakr, and they had three sons: Hamdir, Sorli, and Erp. Yet as Brynhild had predicted,

Above: One Norse belief was that the armor worn by the Valkyries on their divine errands caused the flickering northern lights, aurora borealis.

each of Gudrún's children were to die tragically. First, King Jormunrek killed Svanhild, Gudrún and Sigurd's daughter. In revenge, Gudrún sent her three sons to avenge Svanhild's death, but all were killed, and Brynhild was finally avenged.

The Valkyries in Opera

Most Valkyrie myths involved prophecy, battles, death, betrayal, jealousy, rage, and tragedy, so they lend themselves well to theatrical interpretations. In the late 19th century the major Norse myths, including the *Völsunga Saga*, were adapted by German composer Richard Wagner (1813–1883) for use in his cycle of four operas, collectively titled *Der Ring des Nibelungen* ("The Ring of the Nibelungs"). The second opera in the cycle is *Die Walküre* ("The Valkyries") and features Brunhild (Brynhild), who is a central character in the rest of the cycle.

ALYS CAVINESS

The Prose and Poetic Eddas

Two written collections, the *Poetic Edda* and the *Prose Edda*, are among the most important sources of Scandinavian myth. Scholars believe that the *Poetic Edda* (also known as the *Elder Edda*) was composed between 800 and 1100 CE; it was preserved in the medieval manuscript known as the Codex Regius (c. 1270). The *Poetic Edda* is divided into a mythological section describing the Aesir (one major group of gods), and a heroic section, which included the legend of Sigurd and the destruction of the royal family of Gjúkung.

Icelandic scholar Snorri Sturluson (1179–1241) wrote the *Prose Edda*. It was divided into three sections: "Gylfaginning" ("Beguiling of Gylfi"), "Skáldskaparmál" ("Language of Poetry"), and "Hattatal" ("Catalog of Meters"). "Gylfaginning" and "Skáldskaparmál" contained myths about creation, gods, giants, dwarfs, and Ragnarok. Brynhild is one of the Valkyries named in the two *Eddas*.

Bibliography
Byock, Jesse L., trans. *The Saga of the Volsungs: The Norse Epic of Sigurd the Dragon Slayer.* Berkeley, CA: University of California Press, 2002.
Davidson, H. R. Ellis. *Gods and Myths of Northern Europe.* New York: Viking Press, 1990.
Wagner, Richard; Nicholas John, ed.; and Andrew Porter, trans. *The Valkyrie.* New York: Riverrun Press, 1988.

SEE ALSO: Apocalypse Myths; Celts; Demigods and Heroes; Dragons; Freya; Medea; Nibelungs; Odin; Scandinavia; Sigurd.

VANIR

The Vanir was a group of Scandinavian deities principally associated with abundance, agriculture, fertility, pleasure, and seasonal cycles. The name *Vanir* is thought to be derived from the old Norse word *vinr*, meaning "friend."

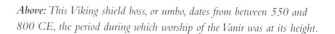

T he Vanir was one of two main groups of Norse gods; the other was the Aesir. Tales of the Aesir predominate in Scandinavian mythology, mainly because its gods were warlike and carried out some of the most bloodthirsty exploits. The Vanir was important, too, however, especially in agriculture, and worship of its deities in Scandinavia is thought to predate that of the Aesir. Vanir gods and goddesses included Bil, Boda, Eir, Fimila, Fjörgyn, Freya, Frimla, Fulla, Gefjon, Gerd, Gná, Hnossa, Hörn, Njörd, Sága, Siguna, Sit, and Vanadís. The goddesses Frigga and Nanna were both Vanir, although they were married to, respectively, Odin and Balder, both Aesir gods. Skadi, wife of Njörd, is also numbered among the Vanir, although she was the daughter of a giant rather than, as would normally be required, the offspring of two deities. The dwelling place of the Vanir was Vanaheim, which was located in Asgard, on the highest level of the universe. There they ruled over the powers of nature, wealth, fertility, and trade. It has been suggested that the peoples who first venerated the Vanir were mariners, since many of the Vanir had special connections with the sea.

Warring pantheons

According to legend, in ancient times there was a war between the Aesir and the Vanir. There are various accounts of the cause of the hostilities. According to one version, they started after members of the Aesir murdered the witch-giant Angrboda, mother of the wolf Fenrir, the

Above: This Viking shield boss, or umbo, dates from between 550 and 800 CE, the period during which worship of the Vanir was at its height.

Midgard Serpent, and Hel. In another account, the war broke out when the Vanir attacked the Aesir because the Aesir had tortured Gullveig, a Vanir priestess or sorceress—her identity is unclear. Outraged, the Vanir issued an ultimatum, demanding either financial recompense or equal status as the Aesir. The Aesir remained defiant, however, and declared war on the Vanir. Whatever started the armed struggle, it went on for many years and could never be settled decisively one way or the other. The Vanir were not naturally warlike, but when they took up arms against the Aesir, they gave as good as they got. At length the conflict ended with a peace treaty and an exchange of hostages. The Vanir sent their leaders—Njörd and his twin son and daughter, Frey and Freya—to live with the Aesir. The trio always maintained strong links with their former kin, however. The Aesir, in turn, sent handsome Hoenir and Mímir, possessor of ancient wisdom, to the Vanir. Hoenir, however, was unable to make any decisions without Mímir's advice, so the Vanir felt cheated. They had sent their very best, while the Aesir had sent Mímir along with an incompetent would-be chief. The Vanir acted with uncharacteristic brutality by cutting off Mímir's head and sending it to the Aesir. Horrified at the loss of so much wisdom, the chief god Odin anointed Mímir's severed head with herbs and worked magic spells so that all the knowledge it contained would be preserved intact, albeit only for Odin's personal use.

To seal the truce at the end of the war, all the deities of the Aesir and the Vanir spat into a jar as a symbol of their reunion. Their saliva was miraculously transformed into Kvasir, the wisest being who ever lived. Kvasir wandered the world, sharing his immense knowledge with everyone he encountered, until finally he came to the home of Fjaler and Galar. These two evil dwarfs became so tired of listening to Kvasir's words of wisdom that they murdered him. Then they mixed his blood with honey and brewed it to make mead. Anyone who drank this liquor would become a poet. The Vanir are thus indirectly involved in the myth of the creation of poetry. However, some sources describe Kvasir as a member of the Aesir; according to others, he was one of the hostages handed over by the Vanir at the end of the war.

Authorities

Some references to Norse religious customs and beliefs are found in the works of Julius Caesar (100–44 BCE) and Roman historian Tacitus (c. 56–120 CE). Most of what we know about early Scandinavian mythology, however, comes from Christian times. One of the most important early authorities is Icelandic author Snorri Sturluson (1179–1241), compiler of the *Prose Edda*. The problem with this work is that, by the time it was written, the legends it described were no longer widely believed. Snorri himself was a Christian, and it is therefore no surprise that his accounts of Nordic mythology are influenced by his knowledge of—and belief in—the Judeo-Christian Bible.

In the *Germania*, Tacitus describes the worship of a goddess, Nerthus, by seven distinct Nordic peoples on an unidentified island in the Baltic Sea. He says that during her annual festival a covered cart, drawn by cattle and led by a priest into a sacred grove, was washed in a hidden lake. The slaves who performed this ritual cleansing were then drowned in order to preserve the secrecy of the ceremony. The name Nerthus—which is not corroborated by other sources of the period—appears to be a corruption of *Njörd*. The change of sex from male Njörd to female Nerthus is inexplicable—it was most likely fortuitous, but some scholars have speculated that originally Nerthus and Njörd may have been separate Vanir deities, and that their relationship might have been similar to that between Greek deities Poseidon and Demeter. Etymologically, the name

Njörd could then be related to that of Greek Nereus, wise old god of the Mediterranean in general and the Aegean Sea in particular.

Little is known about the individual stories of other members of the Vanir, and most of the information we have comes from the work of Snorri. According to him, Bil was one of two children abducted by Máni, the moon, to be his companions. Eir was goddess of healing. Fjörgyn was mother of Thor; her name means "earth," and she is sometimes described as a full-fledged earth mother. Any role that Frigga may have played in the Vanir was eclipsed by her more important function as Odin's wife. Gefjon was a maiden goddess who transformed her four giant sons into oxen, harnessed them, and made them pull Zealand (or Sjaeland) out of Sweden and place it in Denmark, of which it is now a part. Gerd was daughter of the giant Gymir, and wife of Frey. The goddess Gná was Frigg's messenger; she rode across the sea and sky on the back of the magic horse Hófvarpnir. According to Snorri, Nanna was the wife of

Below: This Viking rune stone was inscribed about 800 CE. Its main motifs are a ship, which may be taken as a symbol of the Aesir, and an animal, which may represent the agricultural deities of the Vanir.

Above: *In this painting from the early 20th century by J. Doyle Penrose, Loki is depicted chained to a rock. Above him is a snake that drips venom onto his face. The serpent was put in place by Vanir goddess Skadi.*

The Marriage of Njörd and Skadi

A giant, called Thjazi, had a fair-faced daughter named Skadi. This giantess, known as the Goddess of Snowshoes or the Ski Goddess, loved living at her father's homestead in the mountains of Thrymheim, where she skied and hunted wild animals with her bow and arrows. After the Aesir killed her father for stealing the golden apples of immortality, Skadi stormed off to their home in Asgard to take revenge. She was a formidable sight and the Aesir backed away, offering her a husband in compensation. They promised that she could have any unmarried god she chose. She hoped for the fair Balder, whom all women adored, but the Aesir decreed that she would have to base her choice on the gods' feet alone. She chose the cleanest and whitest, certain that they must be Balder's.

They belonged instead to Njörd, the sea god, whose feet were always being washed and caressed by the sea. Skadi was disappointed, but she agreed to the bargain. Njörd came from Nóatún—the name means "ship enclosure" in Old Norse—a seaside region that he always regarded as home. When the couple married, Skadi tried to persuade her husband to live in her family home, but Njörd could not abide being cut off from the sea. Skadi, however, hated the coast with equal passion.

According to Snorri Sturluson, Njörd and Skadi tried to resolve this difficulty by spending nine nights in Thrymheim and then nine nights in Nóatún. Even this compromise did not work, however: Njörd could not bear the howling of the wolves (he preferred the whooping of swans); for her part, Skadi could not stand the screaming of seagulls, which she thought deliberately returned to land every morning to stop her

Above: This undated drawing shows Vanir god Njörd conducting his bride, Skadi, to his home by the sea.

from sleeping. Their differences were irreconcilable. Skadi retired to the hills.

Later, Skadi played a role in another famous episode in Norse mythology. When the trickster god Loki was captured and bound by the gods of the Aesir, Skadi fastened a venomous snake over his face.

Balder; at his funeral she collapsed and died of grief, and her body was placed with that of her husband on the funeral pyre. However, in the version of the legend recounted by Danish historian Saxo Grammaticus (c. 1150–after 1216), Nanna was married to Höd, Balder's brother and killer. The goddess Saga lived at Sökkvabekk, described by Snorri only as "a big place." Skadi was the giant wife of sea god Njörd. In order to avenge the murder of her father, Thjazi, by Thor, Skadi took up arms against the Aesir. The Aesir, wanting to appease her anger, offered her the choice of one of their number for a husband, with the stipulation that she choose a god by his legs (or feet) alone. She chose Njörd, thinking that he was the fair god Balder. Their marriage went ahead, but was doomed to failure because Njörd preferred to live by the sea, while Skadi was happier in Thrymheim, her father's home in

the mountains. In some sources, Skadi was known as the goddess of snowshoes (see box, above). Another tradition relates that Skadi later married Odin and bore him sons.

KATHLEEN JENKS

Bibliography
Larrington, Carolyne, trans. *The Poetic Edda*. New York: Oxford University Press, 1996.
Lindow, John. *Norse Mythology: A Guide to the Gods, Heroes, Rituals, and Beliefs*. New York: Oxford University Press, 2002.
Simek, Rudolf, and Angela Hall, trans. *A Dictionary of Northern Mythology*. Rochester, NY: Boydell and Brewer, 1993.
Snorri Sturluson, and Anthony Faulkes, trans. *Edda*. New York: Oxford University Press, 1991.

SEE ALSO: Aesir; Balder; Frey; Freya; Frigga; Gefjon; Kvasir; Loki; Njörd; Odin; Scandinavia; Thor.

VENUS

Venus was the Roman goddess of love. From at least as early as the fourth century BCE she was identified with Greek goddess Aphrodite. Almost all of the myths attached to the Roman goddess were inherited from her Greek counterpart.

Left: The Capitoline Venus, by an unknown Roman artist, is based on an earlier statue of Aphrodite by Greek sculptor Praxiteles (370–330 BCE).

Venus was the lover of Mars, the Roman war god who was identified with the Greek Ares, and the wife of Vulcan, the equivalent of the Greek Hephaestus. Another important relationship Venus enjoyed was with a Trojan prince named Anchises. The goddess fell in love with the mortal when she saw him tending his flocks on Mount Ida, and she eventually bore him a son, Aeneas. According to myth, Aeneas grew up to found the city of Rome. As Aeneas's mother, Venus enjoyed a special place in the Roman pantheon.

However, for all the importance attached to her, the origins of the Roman Venus still remain unclear. There is no evidence of her in the earliest Roman religious calendars, and, unlike a number of the old Roman gods, she had no flamen (a type of priest dedicated entirely to the worship of a single deity). Two Roman writers, Marcus Terentius Varro (116–27 BCE) and Ambrosius Theodosius Macrobius (fl. c. 400 CE), remark upon her absence in archaic religious sources. This lack of evidence has led many scholars to conclude that Venus was not an early Roman divinity at all.

The oldest existing representation of Venus is an engraving on a mirror found in the ancient Italian city of Praeneste (present-day Palestrina). It dates from the second half of the fourth century BCE, and the goddess is labeled Venos, an archaic spelling of *Venus*. She is seated to the left of Jupiter; to his right is Proserpina, the goddess of the dead. The three gods are grouped around a small ornamental box, the burial chest of Venus's young lover, Adonis. Jupiter has been called in to arbitrate the

Above: Birth of Venus *by Sandro Botticelli (1445–1510) depicts the goddess rising from the waves. Like most myths about Venus, the story of her birth was originally told about her Greek counterpart, Aphrodite.*

competing claims of the two goddesses, both of whom are in love with Adonis. Venus wants Adonis to live with her, while Proserpina claims him for the underworld. Jupiter's compromise is to allow Adonis to spend four months of every year with Venus, four months with Proserpina, and four months to do as he pleases. The compromise distresses Venus, who in the engraving covers her face with her cloak. Thus the very first visual image of Venus is a reference to a myth that was originally attached to the Greek Aphrodite, evidence that the two goddesses were synonymous from a very early age.

Venus, goddess of gardens

The first explicit mention of Venus in Roman literature dates from around the mid-third century BCE, when author Gnaeus Naevius (c. 270–c. 199 BCE) used her name symbolically to stand for green vegetables. This association was echoed in the second century BCE, when comic writer Titus Maccius Plautus (c. 254–184 BCE) referred to Venus as the protector of gardens. Varro wrote that vegetable growers made August 19 a holiday "because on that date a temple was dedicated to Venus and gardens were sacred to her." In his summary of the work of first-century-CE scholar Marcus Verrius Flaccus, Sextus Pompeius Festus (second or third century CE) explicitly states that gardens were under the watchful protection of Venus. These

passages might seem to suggest that Venus was originally a Roman goddess of gardens. This theory has largely been rejected by modern scholars, however. Some have suggested that the fact that statues of Venus graced Roman gardens may indicate that her physical beauty was thought to have the power to draw out the life-giving forces of growth. According to this interpretation, Venus's role as the protective goddess of gardens would have been secondary to her primary role as goddess of love.

Venus's rise in status can be seen in the number and magnificence of the temples that were established in her

The Name of Venus

Since the publication in 1954 of *La Religion Romaine de Vénus,* a study by academic Robert Schilling, scholars have tried to establish the meaning of the goddess's name as revealed through a cluster of Latin words related to *Venus.* The Latin verb *venerari* means "to venerate or solicit the good will of a god." The noun *veneratio* denotes "the act of worship, or veneration." The noun *venia* denotes a "kindly or charming disposition" and often "forgiveness" sought through worship of the gods. The term *venenum* refers to an herb or potion—especially a love charm—used for medicinal or magical purposes. An underlying meaning in all these words is "charm," perhaps even "magical charm." When a Roman "venerated" a god or goddess, he intended to capture the deity's good will (*venia*) and to "charm" the deity, thus winning the god's or goddess's assent to his prayer.

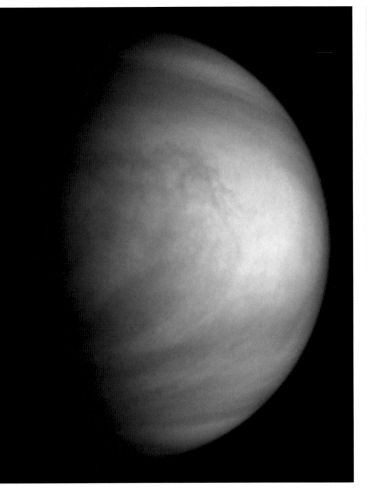

Venus and Purification

The idea that Venus was closely associated with the process of purification is indicated by her association with three goddesses. To begin with, she was identified with Mefitis, a goddess of the sulfurous fumes that arose from the earth. Sulfur was used in ritual as a purifying and healing agent. Both Mefitis and Venus were given the epithet *Fisica,* a Roman form of the Greek *physika,* meaning "concerned with nature." Venus was also associated with the goddess Cloacina, whose name is based on a root meaning "to cleanse." One purifying ritual celebrated by the Romans and Sabines involved fumigation by incense. It was performed on a spot where the statues of Venus and Cloacina later stood. The fact that purifying rituals were used in Roman funerals may account for the fact that Venus was also associated with Libitina, the goddess of undertakers.

Baths, which included the process of purification with incense, were a feature of Venus's rituals. On April 1 the statue of Venus was ritually undressed and bathed, after which her attendants bedecked her anew with robes and jewels in great solemnity.

Left: One of the brightest objects in the night sky, the planet Venus was named for the Roman goddess of love.

honor from the middle of the Republican period (509–31 BCE) onward. The first temple of Venus in Rome was erected in 295 BCE by politician Quintus Fabius Maximus. It stood near the Circus Maximus. According to Roman writer Livy (59 BC–17 CE), it was paid for by fines levied on Roman matrons convicted of adultery. There the goddess was worshiped as Venus Obsequens, a name that suggests she looked favorably on peoples' prayers. The temple was dedicated on August 19 during the Rustic Vinalia, a wine festival that was originally associated purely with Jupiter but was eventually shared with Venus. Venus gradually took on an expanded role in Roman festivals, from which she had originally been absent, and came to be closely associated with Jupiter.

Venus of Mount Eryx

Venus's close relationship with the father of the gods was strengthened in 215 BCE when Quintus Fabius Maximus (d. 203 BCE), the grandson of Quintus Fabius Maximus, dedicated a temple to Venus on the Capitoline Hill. The new temple was built close to the great sanctuary of Jupiter Optimus Maximus. The dedication day of Venus's temple was April 23, a date that coincided with the Earlier Vinalia, another wine festival that was originally sacred to Jupiter alone. The new Capitoline temple housed the cult of Venus of Mount Eryx. The cult, which had been imported from Sicily, incorporated both Greek and Phoenician elements and emphasized pleasure and fertility. In Sicily the cult had flourished among the Elymians, a people who considered themselves, like the Romans, to be Trojan immigrants. The importation of the cult thus emphasized the ties between Aeneas, Venus, and Rome. In contrast to the Sicilian rites, however, the rituals carried out in the new temple in Rome were performed with decorum and reserve.

A second Roman sanctuary of Venus Erycina (from Eryx, modern Erice in Sicily) was dedicated by Porcius Licinius in 181 BCE outside the Colline Gate. It was renowned for its elegant temple and surrounding colonnade. Both Ovid (43 BCE–17 CE) and Plutarch (c. 46–120 CE) described the rituals performed at the new temple, which were closer in spirit to those celebrated on Mount Eryx.

The foundation story of the temple of Venus Verticordia ("Venus the Changer of Hearts"), built on the slope of Rome's Aventine Hill in 114 BCE, emphasizes the

Above: The Temple of Venus in the ground of the villa of Emperor Hadrian. The temple dates from the first century BCE.

goddess's respect for chastity. The sanctuary was built as an act of atonement for the moral lapse of three vestal virgins who had broken their vow of chastity. A woman named Sulpicia, judged to be the most virtuous matron of Rome, was selected to dedicate the goddess's cult statue. The foundation myth of the Venus Verticordia cult expresses the traditionally Roman character of the goddess, which contrasts with the more eastern, Greek and Phoenician, nature of the Venus of Mount Eryx. It seems likely that the character of the Roman Venus was largely formed in the Latin religious sanctuary near the city of Lavinium (modern Pratica di Mare), where she was worshiped in association with Aeneas.

A number of Roman statesmen took steps to be associated with either Venus or her Greek predecessor. In the early first century BCE the general Lucius Cornelius Sulla (138–78 BCE) assumed the nickname Epaphroditus ("Beloved of Aphrodite") to assert that he was her favorite. In 55 BCE another Roman general, Pompey the Great

(106–48 BCE), dedicated a temple to Venus Victrix ("Venus, Granter of Victory") on the Campus Martius. Later, Roman general and political leader Julius Caesar (100–44 BCE) built a temple to Venus Genetrix ("Venus the Mother"). The inference was that Venus was the mother of both Caesar's family and the Roman people as a whole. Caesar's successor as emperor and adopted son, Augustus (63 BCE–14 CE), allotted Venus a place in the temple of Mars. Later, Emperor Hadrian (76–138 CE) supervised the construction of the Temple of Venus and Roma. The temple was dedicated on April 21, the traditional date for the founding of Rome. The choice of this date strengthened the identification of Venus with Rome itself.

DANIEL P. HARMON

Bibliography

Scheid, John, and Janet Lloyd, trans. *An Introduction to Roman Religion*. Bloomington IN: Indiana University Press, 2003.
Turcan, Robert, and Antonia Nevill, trans. *The Gods of Ancient Rome: Religion in Everyday Life from Archaic to Imperial Times*. New York: Routledge, 2001.

SEE ALSO: Aeneas; Aphrodite; Jupiter; Rome.

VESTA

Vesta was the Roman goddess of the hearth, the equivalent of the Greek goddess Hestia. Vesta featured in few myths, but she was an important member of the Roman pantheon. Her worship was a central feature of Roman life.

Vesta was the daughter of the fertility god Saturn and his wife Ops, goddess of abundance and wealth. Vesta was the sister of five major Roman deities: Ceres, Plutus, Juno, Neptune, and Jupiter. Unlike her siblings, Vesta appeared in very few stories. One of the few myths to involve her also features Priapus, a minor Roman deity associated with sexuality. Vesta was famous for her chastity. Knowing this, the ever lustful Priapus crept up on her while she was sleeping, hoping to take her by surprise and rape her. However, Vesta was awoken by the braying of the donkey owned by the old satyr Silenus. Thanks to this intervention, Vesta managed to escape from Priapus and preserve her virginity. From that moment on, Vesta was associated with donkeys.

The worship of Vesta

Vesta was one of the more mysterious goddesses of the Roman pantheon. Scholars do not know much about her roots, except that originally Romans worshiped her privately in their own homes. However, the nature of Vesta's cult changed and eventually she was worshiped at a state level. The transformation is attributed to Roman king Numa Pompilius (c. 715–673 BCE), who elevated her status and assigned Rome's safety to her care.

Every Roman household dedicated its hearth to Vesta, and a number of domestic rituals were held in her honor. For example, newborn babies were carried around the family hearth to mark their arrival into the world. Every meal began and ended with an offering to Vesta, usually in the form of the first and last drink of wine.

However, rituals were not restricted to domestic hearths. Every Roman town or city also had a public hearth. The hearth fire of every new colony was kindled with coals brought from the home city of the new arrivals. The flames of Vesta's sacred hearth fires were not allowed to go out. These fires symbolized the spiritual heart of the cities.

In Rome, the sacred fire was kept in the Temple of Vesta (or Aedes Vesta) in the Forum Romanum. The forum was located just to the north of the Palatine Hill, one of the seven hills of Rome. Historians believed that a succession of temples was built on this site. The one that remains today dates from 191 CE, when Julia Domna (c. 167–217 CE), wife of Roman emperor Septimius Severus (c. 145–211 CE), ordered its restoration. She had 20 columns built around the central circular room and the outer walls decorated with half columns. The sacred hearth burned at the very center of the building, where it was tended by six priestesses known as the vestal virgins. According to legend, this flame was first ignited in the seventh century BCE during the reign of Numa Pompilius. It represented Rome's security and prosperity. Every year on March 1 the fire was ceremoniously renewed. The sacred fire in Vesta's temple burned until 394 CE, when the temple was closed by Emperor Theodosius (347–395 BCE) as part of a purge of all non-Christian cults.

The Temple of Vesta played an important role in the festival of Vestalia, which lasted for a week, beginning on June 7 and ending on June 15. Normally, the inner sanctum of the temple could only be visited by the vestal virgins. However, on the first day of the festival it opened its doors to all female citizens of Rome. The women visited the temple barefoot and made offerings to the goddess. On the last day of the festival, the vestal virgins ritually cleansed the temple.

The vestal virgins were the only female priests within the Roman religious system. They came under the protection of the Pontifex Maximus (the high priest of Rome), and were led by the Virgo Vestalis Maxima, the most senior vestal virgin. Girls were selected to be vestal

Right: The Vestal Virgin *by German artist Alois Schram (1864–1919). The vestal virgins, priestesses who dedicated their lives to Vesta, played an important role in Roman religion.*

Above: The Vestal Virgins *by Hector Leroux (1829–1900). The painting depicts a ceremony being carried out at the Temple of Vesta in the Forum Romanum.*

Portrayal in Art

Although few ancient representations of Vesta survive today, scholars believe that she was usually depicted as a stern woman wearing a long dress with her head covered. She was seen as being regal and removed. Her personality stood in contrast to that of other Roman deities, who were more human in nature, and whose exploits involved interaction with mortals. The absence of stories and myths involving the goddess may account for the paucity of paintings and statues depicting her.

Although Vesta herself is not particularly widely represented in art, her attendants, the vestal virgins, have been a relatively more popular subject. One of the most famous depictions of one of Vesta's priestesses is *Herm of a Vestal Virgin*, a marble bust by Italian sculptor Antonio Canova (1757–1822). The bust has a sparse appearance that reflects the strict morality of the order—the white of the marble suggests the vestal virgin's purity. The priestess is depicted gazing coldly into the distance with a scarf wrapped around her hair.

virgins between the ages of six and ten. The girls were chosen by the Pontifex Maximus and came from distinguished patrician families—the patricians were the wealthier of the two classes of Roman citizens, the other class being the plebeians. Vestal virgins served for 30 years: the first 10 years as novices, the next 10 years as vestal virgins proper, and the last 10 years as tutors to the younger priestesses. After 30 years of service, they were released from their vow of chastity and allowed to marry.

The vestal virgins enjoyed privileges that other Roman women did not. They could own their own property, for example. They also had special front-row seats at games—all other women were relegated to the back rows. However, if a vestal virgin broke her vow of chastity, she could expect a harsh punishment. The blood of vestal virgins could not be spilled, so transgressors were buried alive. The offender's lover was flogged to death. The live burials took place at the Campus Sceleratus ("evil field"), located outside the Servian Wall that surrounded Rome. These executions were infrequent, but several did occur.

Vestal virgins in myth

One of the most famous mythical vestal virgins was Rhea Silvia, daughter of King Numitor of Alba Longa, who was dethroned by his brother Amulius. Amulius ordered the Pontifex Maximus to choose his niece for service to Vesta;

House of the Vestal Virgins

From the sixth century BCE until the end of the fourth century CE, Vesta's priestesses lived together in the House of the Vestal Virgins (or Atrium Vestae). The House of the Vestal Virgins was located behind the Temple of Vesta, between the Palatine Hill and the Regia (the residence of the kings of Rome). Together, the Temple of Vesta, the House of the Vestal Virgins, the Regia, and another building called the Domus Publica formed a complex where all the religious duties of the king were carried out. Scholars believe that the king's wife and daughters administered the cult of Vesta until Rome became a republic.

An older House of the Vestal Virgins, smaller than the present ruins, was aligned on an east–west axis. It consisted of a front room that ran the full width of the house on the north side and six separate rooms in the back. This floor plan was maintained for over five centuries, until 64 CE, when the building was destroyed by fire. The ruins that are visible today are the remains of the building that was built after the fire. The new house was larger and had three levels. Scholars believe the vestal virgins' private rooms were on the first floor. The house contained statues of former vestal virgins. After the suppression of all non-Christian cults in 394 CE, the vestal virgins were forced to leave the complex, and the sacred fire was extinguished.

Right: The remains of the House of the Vestal Virgins in Rome. The statues depict former vestal virgins and date from around the beginning of the third century CE.

he had learned from an oracle that Rhea Silvia's children would threaten his power. Rhea Silvia served Vesta faithfully as a vestal virgin, until one day she was raped by Mars, Roman god of war. In due course, Rhea Silvia gave birth to twin boys, Romulus and Remus. Fearing the prophecy, Amulius abandoned the boys on the Tiber River. However, they survived and grew up to overthrow Amulius and found the city of Rome.

Another famous mythical vestal virgin was Julia Flammia, who was chosen to be a virgin when she was nine years old. The only memento she possessed from her childhood was her mother's plain agate necklace. One day, while the young priestess was tending the sacred fire, the necklace broke and the beads fell into the flames. Julia fished them out with an iron rod and discovered that the stones had become the color of the fire. The Romans used this myth to explain the origins of carnelian, a red semiprecious stone.

ALYS CAVINESS

Bibliography

Gardner, Jane F. *Roman Myths.* Austin, TX: University of Texas Press, 1994.

Scheid, John, and Janet Lloyd, trans. *An Introduction to Roman Religion.* Bloomington, IN: Indiana University Press, 2003.

Turcan, Robert, and Antonia Nevill, trans. *The Gods of Ancient Rome: Religion in Everyday Life from Archaic to Imperial Times.* New York: Routledge, 2001.

SEE ALSO: Hestia; Priests and Priestesses; Rhea Silvia; Rome; Romulus and Remus; Virginity.

VIRGINITY

Since ancient times virginity has been of profound importance in many cultures. Its modern definition is more certain than the various definitions it had in different parts of the ancient world. More recently virginity has been associated with words such as *maiden;* but a maiden or a virgin has not always been someone who has never engaged in sex.

The concept of virginity is complicated: it encompasses many areas of belief, such as sexual activity, conception, rebirth, and ritual purity. Some Western assumptions about the concept of virginity are that it is common to all cultures, and that a virgin is a person of either sex who has never engaged in sexual intercourse. It is often assumed that terms or concepts meaning the same as the English word *virgin* can be found in most languages. However, in some cultures, such as that of the ancient Egyptians, there seems to have been no equivalent term. The pharaonic Egyptians made a distinction between young women who had given birth and those who had never had children, rather than those who had or had not engaged in sexual activity. The English word *virgin* comes from a Latin word, *virgo*, which simply means "young woman." The ancient Greek word *parthenos* was used to describe a young woman who had not given birth, but it did not indicate if the woman had ever had sex.

The qualities that ancient societies believed were represented by virginity included purity, youth, faithfulness, and single-mindedness. Many scholars argue that the importance given to virginity in ancient cultures stems from the fact that it was considered to be irreplaceable. However, in the ancient Greek world, or at least among the ancient Greek gods, virginity could be a renewable quality.

For example, the goddess Hera, wife of Zeus, was claimed to have renewed her virgin status each year by bathing in a special stream. There are also references in Greek mythology to women described as *parthenos* who had given birth but who had kept the birth a secret.

Virginity and marriage in the ancient world

In ancient Greece and Rome, girls were married at a young age, often during puberty; this was especially true among the wealthier classes. Marriages were often arrangements between families—not individuals—and were frequently made to cement political alliances or transfer property. It was not considered appropriate for young people to choose their future partners, especially not for girls. In Greece, young girls were also kept secluded—away from men outside the family. There was little chance for a young free woman to engage in sex before marriage. In this ordered society, an unmarried female was most likely to be a young and sexually inexperienced girl. Other than by the word of the guardian family, or from the person who was to be married, there was no precise way to determine if someone was a virgin in the modern sense of the word. For a Greek or Roman girl it was usually considered sufficient proof of her virginity if she was not pregnant.

One factor that helped maintain the central role of virginity in many ancient societies was the concept of ritual purity. Women who had not engaged in sexual activity were believed to be physically and spiritually pure, and they were often regarded as portents of good luck. Various deities in most pantheons embodied these ideas, which were also reinforced by myths that recounted episodes in which virginity was upheld, protected, and fought over.

Virginity in classical mythology

In many Greek and Roman myths there are accounts of gods in love with lesser goddesses, such as nymphs, and with mortal women. Some women welcomed their advances, but most spurned them, often resulting in rape. Although accounts of Zeus's exploits with women are most popular in Greek mythology, Apollo, god of divination, also lusted after many women. For example,

Daphne, a beautiful nymph, was a virgin huntress. When Apollo saw Daphne he immediately fell in love. However, Apollo's persistent sexual advances frightened Daphne, and she was worried that he was going to rape her. In desperation she fled from Apollo and prayed for help to her father, the river god Peneius (or in some versions to Gaia, the earth goddess). Daphne's prayers were answered and she was turned into a laurel tree; her virginity was protected. From that point on Apollo wore a laurel leaf as a symbol of his love for Daphne.

Above: An exchange of rings during the Roman wedding ceremony is depicted in this second-century-CE marble relief. The bride (center) is shown receiving her ring.

Some scholars consider Mount Olympus, the home of the Greek gods, to be the origin of the modern concept of virginity. There virgin goddesses did not give birth, and they did not have sexual relations with gods or mortals. The three Olympian goddesses who successfully avoided sex were Hestia (the Roman Vesta), Athena, and Artemis.

Cassandra

Cassandra was a Trojan virgin priestess. Early myths about her recount that she was courted by the god Apollo, who offered her the ability to see the future if she would sleep with him. She agreed, but after she had learned to see the future she refused to keep to her side of the agreement. Apollo then cursed her so that her foresight would never be believed. Cassandra remained a virgin until the Trojan War, when the Greek hero Ajax raped her. After Troy fell to the Greeks, she became a captive of Agamemnon, the Greek leader. He also raped her and kept her as his concubine. In *Agamemnon*, a play by Aeschylus (525–456 BCE), the virgin goddess Athena punishes the Greeks for the rape of Cassandra by sending storms to hamper their departure from the sacked city of Troy.

Above: In this Roman fresco (c. 79 BC) from Pompeii, Cassandra is trying in vain to warn the Trojans of the imminent arrival of the Greeks. She was cursed never to be believed, however.

Hestia

Hestia was the first-born child of Rhea and her brother, the Titan Cronus. Cronus feared being overthrown by one of his children, so he swallowed them all at birth. When Zeus was born, however, Rhea gave her husband a stone swaddled in cloth to eat and stole the child away to Crete. When he grew up, Zeus returned to Olympus and overthrew his father, forcing him to regurgitate the other children. Cronus's children emerged from their father's stomach in the reverse order to which they had been swallowed. Accordingly, Hestia became the youngest child. During her youth she was approached by Poseidon and Apollo, but she refused their proposals. She renounced marriage and finally swore an oath of chastity. Zeus was pleased by this and appointed her goddess of the hearth.

Every Greek home had a central hearth or fireplace. In a small house this would be not only the place for cooking, but also the only means of heating in winter. Larger houses might have several hearths. Of all the Olympians, Hestia was thus the most essential to everyday life, and yet she was the most overlooked by artists, poets, and writers. Hardly any ancient pictures of Hestia exist, and there are few hymns to her. She is mentioned in only a few myths, and there were no temples built in her honor. However, she was worshiped in every home, and her Roman equivalent, Vesta, was worshiped by an order of priestesses called the vestal virgins.

Athena

Athena was perhaps the least feminine of the Greek virgin goddesses. Born from the head of Zeus, she represented qualities such as cunning and skill. She had no mother and no fellow-feeling for female deities or mortals; in one myth she even says that she will always take the side of men rather than women. Representations of Athena in classical Greek art are warlike and often depict her with a shield, a spear, and a helmet. However, in various myths she was the patron of weaving and spinning—activities that were usually associated with women in the ancient world.

In Rome, Athena was known as Minerva. Minerva was originally a distinct goddess from Athena, although they shared similar qualities. Minerva was the daughter of the supreme god of the original Roman pantheon, Jupiter, and was a perpetual virgin goddess—although there is one Roman myth in which she was the mother of the Muses, goddesses who personified the arts and sciences. (In this account, the Muses' father was said to be Jupiter, which would also have made him their grandfather). In Greek mythology the Muses were more often described as the

Below: Greek sculptor Alcamenes (fifth century BCE) is thought to have sculpted the original bronze statue of the virgin goddess Athena, from which this first-century-CE copy was made.

daughters of
Mnemosyne. Minerva's
connection with them
probably springs from the
belief that she invented
musical instruments, and from
her annual celebrations, in which
instruments were purified in her temple.
Over time the personalities of Athena and
Minerva merged. For the Romans it seems that Minerva
was a patron of weaving and spinning, as well as the
personification of cunning, intelligence, and skill. Minerva
also fulfilled some of the functions that were satisfied by
Apollo in Greek beliefs. Those who wanted to be successful
in sculpting, painting, poetry, and medicine prayed to her;
for the Greeks, Apollo was the father of Asclepius, the god
of medicine.

Artemis

In Greek myth Artemis was the twin of Apollo. According
to some myths, Artemis was born first and helped to deliver
her brother. She was the virgin goddess of hunting, and
protector of women in childbirth. In some myths she was
a moon goddess, and her associations with animals and
the hunt also earned her the title Mistress of the Animals.
Scholars suggest that one reason for Artemis's many titles
is that over time she absorbed the responsibilities of other
goddesses and had other functions projected on to her by
her worshipers. Sometimes traces of these other goddesses
can be seen in the names given to Artemis at various sites
of worship. For example, in the city of Ephesus (in modern
Turkey) she was worshiped as a fertility deity. Statues of
her from the area, including *Diana of Ephesus* (Artemis
was known as Diana in Rome), show the goddess wearing
a ritual garment adorned with horned animals and a
crown. It was originally thought that the statue's multiple
breasts symbolized Artemis's aspect as a fertility goddess.
However, modern scholars suggest that these are
representations of bull testicles draped over the goddess.
Romans saw the bull as a symbol of male fertility, and it
was not unusual for a female fertility goddess to be
associated with male fertility.

In some myths Artemis is combined with other virgin
goddesses, and in others she is their champion. Britomartis,
for example, was a semidivine devotee of Artemis from the

Above: A statue in Syracuse, Sicily, shows the river god Alpheus peering at the nymph Arethusa from behind the standing figure of Artemis. Artemis's virgin companion, Arethusa was pursued by Alpheus, the god of the river in which she was bathing. Artemis transformed Arethusa into a spring to protect her from being raped.

island of Crete. She was the daughter of Zeus by a mortal woman. Minos, king of Crete, desired her so much that he chased her to the edge of a cliff. Rather than be raped by Minos, Britomartis jumped into the sea, but she became entangled in fishing nets and nearly drowned. Artemis, however, saved her and made her goddess of hunters and fishers. In other versions Britomartis is identified with Artemis, rather than existing as a separate deity. Although Britomartis was not a major goddess in the classical world, ruins of a magnificent temple dedicated to her still stand on the Greek island of Aegina.

Hippolytus, son of Theseus, is an unusual example in Greek mythology of a man devoted to a virgin goddess. He took a vow of chastity early in his life, devoutly worshiping Artemis; but was punished by Aphrodite, goddess of love, who claimed that he had neglected to worship her. As a punishment Aphrodite caused Phaedra, Hippolytus's stepmother, to fall in love with him. Hippolytus rejected Phaedra's advances, so she falsely accused Hippolytus of rape. Outraged, Theseus prayed to Poseidon for Hippolytus's death. Hippolytus fled after his father's curse, but as he rode away in his chariot, Poseidon sent a bull out of the sea that terrified the horses. The chariot overturned and Hippolytus was caught in the reins and dragged to his death. Another myth claims that, before Hippolytus went to the underworld, Artemis rewarded his life of chastity by spiriting him away to Italy and making him a minor god called Virbius.

Before Rome became a great city that gave its name to an empire, it was a town belonging to the Latins. The Latins and their neighbors, the Sabines, worshiped an advanced form of the goddess Artemis called Diana, virgin goddess of the moon and of remote places. Like Artemis, Diana disliked the company of men, although men were allowed to worship her. Unlike Artemis, Diana seems to have been an only child and was closely associated with slaves. The Romans had a festival called the Day of Slaves, during which Diana was worshiped as their protector.

Vestal virgins and the example of Tuccia

The vestal virgins were an ancient Roman order of priestesses who worshiped Vesta, goddess of the hearth. They were seen to be the holiest women in Rome. They would appear at religious ceremonies and festivals in honor of Vesta. One important duty for vestal virgins was to maintain the fire at the altar of Vesta; Romans believed that Rome was protected for as long as the fire was burning. If it was discovered that a vestal virgin had broken her vow of chastity for any reason, she would be buried alive.

Virgin priestesses

The importance of virginity in classical cultures was underlined by elevating certain virgin women to a high status in society. In ancient Greece some virgin priestesses lived in oracular temples, serving as messengers or otherwise for various deities. Oracles were considered to speak on behalf of the gods, and the spokesperson would often be a priestess. At the Delphic oracle these priestesses were called Pythias. The first Pythia was reported to have been the goddess Themis. Pythias dedicated their lives to prophesying on behalf of the god Apollo.

People of ancient Rome also placed a high value on virginity. Nine upper-class girls, chosen between the ages of six and ten, were dedicated to the service of the goddess Vesta. They were contracted to serve her as priestesses for 30 years, during which they could not marry or have sexual intercourse. These priestesses were so holy that if a condemned prisoner crossed their path, the prisoner had to be freed. It was believed that if one of the priestesses broke her vows of virginity, disaster would come to Rome, and several times when there were serious natural catastrophes or wars, the authorities investigated whether a vestal virgin had broken her vows. Because the fate of the city was linked to the virginity of the priestesses, breaking the vows was punishable by death. The transgressor was buried alive in an underground chamber, with a small supply of food. The last vestal virgin to be buried alive was recorded in Roman history; she was killed c. 140 CE, over a hundred years after the birth of Christ.

Virgins who had dedicated their lives to the worship of a god or a goddess were generally considered to be trustworthy, since they were not tied to earthly responsibilities or to their families; their loyalty could not be distracted by familial demands. However, protecting their virginity could sometimes be difficult. For example, Pythias were traditionally young girls, but rape among their order meant that they were replaced by old women, who were less sexually attractive.

Above: Located in the Roman Forum, these ruins were once part of the Temple of Vesta, Roman goddess of the hearth. The forum was the political, economic, and religious center of Rome during the Roman Republic (509–31 BCE).

One Roman legend tells of a vestal virgin who went to great lengths to prove her virginity. Her name was Tuccia, and like all vestals she came from an upper-class Roman family (see box, above). She was unfairly accused of having had sex with a close family member. Since breaking a vestal vow and committing incest were two of the worst crimes in ancient Roman society, the charges were the most severe that could be leveled against anybody. The charges were so severe that a special test was devised to give Tuccia a chance of survival. She was ordered to carry water in a sieve. Tuccia prayed to the goddess Vesta to help her prove her innocence. The goddess appeared to Tuccia and advised her that she would pass the test if she blocked the holes of the sieve with clay. Tuccia followed the goddess's instructions and carried the sieve without spilling any water, thus escaping punishment.

Virginity in Celtic mythology

In one Welsh myth there was a female figure called Arianrhod, whose name means "silver wheel." She was associated with the moon, virginity, and women in general. She was one of the descendants of the goddess Don,

Galahad

Arthurian legend has a special place for the virgin warrior. According to some scholars, the original King Arthur was a real man, who ruled Britain in the late fifth and early sixth centuries. He was then assimilated into Celtic myth and remained popular until the Middle Ages (c. 500–1500 CE), when two major revisions occurred which created the Arthurian legends in existence today. The first, in the 12th century, was the writing of a Latin history of the kings of Britain by Geoffrey of Monmouth (c. 1100–1154). In the late 15th century, Thomas Malory (fl. 1470) rewrote the stories in English. This version provided the names of the characters that are familiar today. In his *Le Morte D'Arthur*, Arthur is transformed from a Celtic tribal chieftain, who might have worn a tartan and lived in a fortified house, to a cultured medieval monarch. Another major change to the original Arthur was the Christianization of the stories. The real king lived at a time when Britain was still largely pagan, but the Arthurian legends are full of Christian symbolism and values. Sir Galahad is a prime example of this. He was a knight of the Round Table, who represents ideal chastity. Galahad is the son of Sir Lancelot, who had to flee King Arthur's castle, Camelot, after sleeping with Queen Guinevere. Except for this indiscretion, Lancelot embodied the virtues that were traditionally most important in knighthood, including faithfulness, bravery, and chivalry. Galahad surpassed his father—he had all these virtues plus chastity, which his father could never manage. In the original Welsh version of the legends, Galahad's name was Gwalchafed, which means "Falcon of Summer."

Above: In this medieval manuscript (c.1370–1380) Galahad— who symbolized chastity—is depicted at far left, being introduced to the company of the Round Table.

and she had two brothers, Gilfaethwy and Gwydion. Arianrhod's story is connected with that of her uncle King Math ap Mathonwy, who, unless he was at war, spent his life with his feet resting in a virgin's lap. Gilfaethwy fell in love with Goewin, Math's original virgin, and with the help of his brother, he raped her. When Math discovered this, he punished his nephews by turning them into animals for three years. He then searched for a replacement virgin and selected Arianrhod. During a task Math had devised to test Arianrhod's virginity, she stepped over a symbolic rod and immediately gave birth to two children, proving that she was not a virgin. One child was a boy named Dylan; he became a sea creature who eventually returned to the waves. The other child was a boy whom Gwydion snatched up and hid in a chest. Gwydion later returned Arianrhod's son to her, but she

rejected and cursed the boy, so Gwydion raised the child himself. It is unclear whether King Math ever managed to replace Goewin.

Irish mythology also had a virgin goddess, Brigid (also called Brighid, Brigindo, Brigantia, Brigantis, Bride or Breo Saighead, whose name means "Fiery Arrow" or "Power"). Brigid was worshiped throughout the Celtic lands. She was a "three-fold goddess." This term is thought to indicate that she was sometimes worshiped as one of three aspects or personalities of a greater goddess. Brigid was a patron of poetry and healing, and of fertility, crafts, and martial arts. Brigid's festival was Imbolc, celebrated on the first of February. During her festival Brigid was personified by a bride, a young girl, or a virgin, and she was celebrated as the protector of women in childbirth. In Christian times she became Saint Brigid.

Above: Phaedra and Hippolytus *by French painter Pierre-Narcisse Guérin (1774–1833). Hippolytus, at left, is one of a few men in Greek mythology who takes a vow of chastity.*

Another prominent Celtic virgin was Gailleach, the White Lady. Gailleach drank at dawn from the Well of Youth, which once again transformed her into a young virgin goddess. Like streams that were considered regenerative in Greek mythology, wells were seen to be sacred in Celtic mythology because they arose from *oimbelc* ("in the belly"), the womb of Mother Earth.

One celebrated figure in Celtic mythology who was not a virgin but who did campaign against marriage was Rosmerta, goddess of fire, warmth, and abundance. She was worshiped by the Celts of Gaul. She was a flower queen and also the queen of death. Despite her dislike of matrimony, Rosmerta was the wife of Esus, the messenger god of Celtic mythology, an equivalent to Hermes for the Greeks.

Virginity in Norse mythology

There are few virgin goddesses in Norse mythology, but there are some prominent virgins. The Valkyries, for example, were originally very sinister figures. They were messengers of the chief god Odin, and they chose which warriors were to die. The chosen heroes were gathered up and borne away to Valhalla, the home of Odin's ghostly army. Any maiden who became a Valkyrie would remain immortal and invulnerable as long as she obeyed the gods and remained a virgin. Valkyries were described as young and beautiful, with long, flowing golden hair. They wore gold or silver helmets and bloodred armor, and they carried spears and shields. When Valkyries came to earth they would appear as swans. Legend has it that if they dropped a feather while they were swans, the man who caught it could compel them to return to earth.

LYN GREEN

Bibliography

Ellis, Peter Berresford. *Celtic Myths and Legends*. New York: Carroll and Graf, 2002.

Gardner, Jane F. *Roman Myths*. Austin, TX: University of Texas Press, 1994.

Graves, Robert. *The Greek Myths*. New York: Penguin USA, 1993.

Lindow, John. *Norse Mythology: A Guide to the Gods, Heroes, Rituals, and Beliefs*. New York: Oxford University Press, 2002.

SEE ALSO: Apollo; Artemis; Athena; Britomartis; Cassandra; Daphne; Hestia; Hippolytus; Valkyries; Vesta; Zeus.

WAYLAND

In Germanic legend Wayland was a
famous blacksmith who suffered at the
hands of a cruel king but exacted an
even crueler revenge. The blacksmith,
whose story has parallels in a number
of Greek and Scandinavian myths,
was known in England as Wayland,
in Germany as Weland, and in
Scandinavia as Völund.

According to legend, Wayland and his two brothers,
Slagfid and Egil, were the sons of a king of
Finland. Each of the three brothers married a
Valkyrie, a maiden who served the chief Norse god, Odin,
by selecting dead warriors to go to the heavenly hall of
Valhalla. One day the Valkyrie wives vanished, and the three
men began to search for them. Each took a different path,
and Wayland, lost in his grief, was captured by King Nídud
of Sweden and brought to his court.

The king seized Wayland's sword for himself and gave
one of the blacksmith's golden rings to his daughter,
Bödvild. Nídud then had the smith work in his own forge,
where Wayland was forced to make weapons and tools for
his kidnapper. Nídud's wife, observing the smith's anger
whenever he caught sight of his ring or his sword,
encouraged her husband to greater cruelty. The king cut
the sinews in Wayland's legs, making him lame, and then
sent him to a remote island, where Wayland continued to
work in a forge for his new master.

Wayland plots his revenge
Alone on the island, Wayland was able to plot his revenge.
He first persuaded Nídud's two young sons to visit him in
his forge. The two boys journeyed to the island alone,
without their father's knowledge or permission. They never
made it home: Wayland killed them and made drinking
bowls from their skulls, which he sent to Nídud; he also
made ornaments from their eyes and teeth, which he sent
to Nídud's wife and Bödvild.

Wayland then received a visit from Bödvild herself, who
had brought her gold ring for the smith to mend. Wayland
made the girl drunk on beer and, when she was asleep,
raped her. He then flew away from the island by means
of a magic coat of feathers, which he had made himself.
Before departing for good, however, Wayland appeared
before Nídud to tell the king exactly what he had done
to his children.

Wayland is associated with a number of other legends.
In one, he was the lord of the elves, diminutive spirits
who were often regarded as mischiefs. According to a

*Left: A dwarf blacksmith, or perhaps Wayland himself, is depicted on this
12th-century relief from the side of a baptismal font in Sweden.*

Right: Wayland's Roman equivalent, the smith Vulcan, works at his forge in this painting by Italian artist Pietro da Cortona (1596–1669).

Scandinavian tradition, Wayland was said to be the son of the sea giant Wade. Wade himself was the son of the giantess Wachilt, who in Norse myth had an affair with a king and then went back to live in the sea. Wachilt later stopped the king's ship, mid-journey, by seizing its prow, and announced that she was pregnant with his son. Wade, born to Wachilt and the king, was believed to have waded across the sea that separates two of Denmark's islands while carrying his own son, Wayland, in his arms.

Some versions of the Wayland legend portray the character as a dwarf, linking him to the metalworking dwarfs of Norse mythology. One story relates how the trickster god Loki, to make amends for cutting off the hair of Thor's wife, Sif, persuaded the dwarfs to make a number of invaluable objects for the gods, including Odin's spear, Frey's ship, a new head of hair for Sif, and, most important of all, Thor's magic hammer.

Another Norse myth tells of Odin's attempts to woo a princess called Rind. Odin disguised himself as a smith and arrived at the court of Rind's father. He gave Rind gold rings, but she rejected his advances. He then gave the girl a drugged drink and raped her, leaving her pregnant with his child. So closely does this story resemble that of Wayland that some scholars believe the Wayland legend is related to the cult of Odin, which was popular among Germanic peoples across northern Europe in the first centuries CE.

The myth's sources and references

The story of Wayland is dark and cruel and contains themes of courage, endurance, and retribution that would have appealed to Germanic peoples across northern Europe. All of these peoples seemed to know something of the Wayland legend.

The most important source for the story is the poem "Völundarkvida," which forms part of the 13th-century Icelandic collection known as the *Poetic Edda*. Although we know when the *Poetic Edda* was assembled, it is not certain when or even where individual poems within it were written. It is likely that some date from the 12th century, while others go back much earlier and could have come from Viking settlements as far away as Ireland or Greenland. In addition, references to Wayland in the Anglo-Saxon literature of Britain between the sixth and the ninth centuries suggest that the legend of the smith is very old.

The first reference to Wayland in Anglo-Saxon literature is in the epic poem *Beowulf*, believed to have been written between 700 and 750. In the poem, Beowulf, a prince of the Geats (a tribe in what is now southern Sweden), arrives at the hall of Hrothgar, king of Denmark, to slay the monster Grendel. Beowulf requests of Hrothgar that, if he dies in the ensuing fight, the king send his chain-mail armor back to his own people, since it was made by Wayland, "that far-famed master smith," and is very precious. Toward the end of the poem, when Beowulf—now king of the Geats—lies dying after his final battle with a dragon, he bequeaths his chain-mail shirt to his kinsman, Wiglaf.

Two later Anglo-Saxon poems also contain references to Wayland. The first is "Deor," which scholars think was written during the reign of Saxon king Alfred the Great (ruled 871–899) of Wessex (in southwestern England). In the poem a minstrel compares his own suffering to that of legendary figures, including Wayland's at the hands of King Nídud. The second poem is "Waldere," thought to be written in the 9th or 10th century but of which only fragments survive. This violent poem contains a reference to a sword named Mimming that was made by Wayland.

A carving on a seventh-century whalebone box—known as the Franks Casket—made in Northumbria, England, depicts the lame Wayland working in his island forge. The fame of the Wayland legend is suggested by the other panels on the box, which show the legendary founders of Rome, Romulus and Remus, and the magi bringing gifts to the infant Jesus.

Blacksmiths in myth and legend

Wayland is one of many famous blacksmiths in myths and legends from a number of cultures. In ancient Egyptian myth, the god Ptah was the patron of craftspeople and made the weapons with which the god Horus defeated the evil Seth. In Indian Vedic myth the smith Tvashtri made weapons for the chief god Indra, while the Ossetic smith Kurdalagon forged a sword for the hero Batraz.

Blacksmiths' importance in myth reflected their significant, but enigmatic, status in many cultures. Smiths worked with iron, a material that people held in awe since it could come either from the ground or from the sky, as meteorites. Another reason for smiths' important position in mythology was that theirs was seen as the "first trade," producing tools on which all the other trades depended.

Below: Carved from whalebone, this is a cast of an eighth-century English jewelry box called the Auzon Casket, named for the town in France where it was discovered in the 19th century. The left side of the front shows scenes from the story of Wayland.

The role of blacksmiths sometimes extended beyond the forging of tools, horseshoes, and weapons. In Ethiopian myth blacksmiths were sorcerers who could change into animals. The Kikuyu people of Kenya believed that smiths could cast spells to protect property or to punish thieves. Healing powers were often attributed to smiths, too. An old English tradition tells of a ritual in which seven smiths cured a sick child.

Many ancient peoples regarded smiths as capable of evil. In Indian mythology smiths were often regarded as enemies of the gods, while some European legends portrayed metalworkers as demons, with flames exiting their mouths. In contrast, several other traditions depicted blacksmiths fighting evil. The Christian saint Dunstan, who was a blacksmith and a goldsmith, was one day visited by the devil. Dunstan kept the devil talking until his tongs had become red-hot. He then grabbed the devil with the tongs and would not let go until the devil had promised not to tempt him again.

These associations with evil, and with fighting evil, are both evident in the story of Wayland. The behavior of Nídud was cruel, and the king deserved his punishment. However, Wayland's revenge was cruel, too, and he was a figure who could inspire both admiration and fear.

The story of Wayland finds parallels in a number of Greek myths. Like Wayland, Hephaestus, the Greek god of fire and metalworking, was lame—although unlike the

Wayland's Smithy

The connection between the Wayland legend and England is not only literary but also geographic. A stone burial chamber in Berkshire, southern England, is known as Wayland's Smithy. A legend associated with the site relates how it was haunted by an invisible blacksmith, who, in return for a coin being left on a stone, would forge a new shoe for a traveler's horse. If the traveler looked toward the chamber while the work was being done, however, no horseshoe would appear.

Similar tales occur in Belgium, Germany, and Denmark. English writer Rudyard Kipling (1865–1936) referred to the legend in his book *Puck of Pook's Hill* (1906). In Kipling's story an old, white-bearded Wayland admits that hard times have reduced him to shoeing horses in return for a coin.

Below: This stone chamber is linked to legends of various smiths, but it is best known for Wayland: it is called Wayland's Smithy.

Germanic character, Hephaestus was born disabled and was thrown out of heaven by his mother, Hera, as a result. A further possible association with Greek myth arises with the magical coat of feathers made by Wayland. The episode may be compared with the story of the Athenian inventor Daedalus, who was imprisoned with his son, Icarus, on the island of Crete by King Minos. Father and son escaped from the island using wings that Daedalus made from feathers and wax.

ANDREW CAMPBELL

Bibliography

Cavendish, Richard, ed. *Man, Myth, and Magic.* New York: Marshall Cavendish, 1995.

Davidson, H. R. Ellis. *Scandinavian Mythology.* London: Hamlyn, 1982.

Orchard, Andy. *Cassell's Dictionary of Norse Myth and Legend.* London: Cassell, 1997.

Synge, Ursula. *Weland, Smith of the Gods.* London: The Bodley Head, 1972.

SEE ALSO: Daedalus; Germanic Peoples; Hephaestus; Odin; Ptah; Romulus and Remus; Scandinavia; Valkyries.

YMIR

In Norse mythology, Ymir was the first creature to emerge from the primordial void. He was a Frost Giant who single-handedly gave birth to a race of creatures like himself. He was then killed by the first gods, who used his body to create the physical world.

Norse peoples believed that at the beginning of time, there was nothing in the universe but a gaping void, which they called Ginnungagap. Two worlds formed on either side of the void: a freezing cold world known as Niflheim, which means "Land of Fog," and an unbearably hot and fiery world known as Muspelheim, which means "Land of Destroyers." In the void, the hot air of Muspelheim came into contact with the ice of Niflheim, and the ice began to melt. It was from the melting drops of ice that Ymir came into existence.

Ymir, the first Frost Giant, soon began to produce more of his kind. Since he was the only being, he reproduced by a similar process to parthenogenesis—reproduction without fertilization. While he slept he sweated, and the drops of moisture under his arms turned into a male and a female. The sweat from one of his feet produced another male. From these three offspring descended an entire race of frost giants.

Death and creation

Ymir was then joined by a cow named Audhumla, another creature formed from the melting ice at the meeting of the hot and cold worlds. Ymir welcomed her arrival because she provided him with a source of sustenance, but it was Audhumla's milk that led to his downfall. While Ymir drank it, Audhumla fed on a block of salty ice. Over the course of three days she licked the ice into the shape of a man, a tall and strong individual named Búri. Búri went on to father a son, Bor, who in turn married Bestla, the daughter of another giant. Bor and Bestla themselves produced the first of the Norse deities: Odin, the chief god, and his two brothers, Vili and Vé. It was these three gods who killed Ymir.

Right: Displayed in the Eimar Sculpture Garden in Reykjavík, Iceland, this 20th-century work depicts Ymir feeding from the udders of the cow Audhumla.

Eimar Jonsson 1909

Above: This frozen winter landscape in Finland is typical of the Scandinavian terrain that inspired the mythological realm of Niflheim.

There is no explicit account in any of the sources of how Búri, the grandfather of the gods, produced his son Bor. One suggestion is that, like his son, he married a giant's daughter. Another is that, like Ymir, he produced his son through parthenogenesis. There is, however, a clear reason why the first gods killed the first frost giant: the gods were essentially good, while Ymir was essentially evil. As Snorri Sturluson (1179–1241), the Icelandic historian and chronicler of Norse myths, wrote of Ymir: "In no way do we recognize him as a god; he was wicked, as were all his descendants."

When Odin, Vili, and Vé killed Ymir, so much blood poured out of his body that all but two of his children drowned—the only survivors were the giant Bergelmir and his wife, who managed to escape in a boat and continue the race of frost giants. This violent end of Ymir was followed by an even more violent disposal of his body, but one which the Norse believed created the world in which they lived. According to the myth, Odin and his brothers placed Ymir's body in the middle of Ginnungagap. They made the earth from his flesh, forests from his hair,

mountains from his large bones, and rocks and pebbles from his small bones and teeth. The giant's blood drained from his body and became the oceans, while the gods arched his skull over the earth to form the sky and threw his brains aloft to form clouds. There were two further uses for the giant's corpse. From maggots growing in its flesh the gods created dwarfs, while they used Ymir's eyebrows to erect a barrier that marked off a realm for the giants, Jotunheim, and a realm for humans—who had not yet been created—known as Midgard.

Parallels with other myths

The story of Ymir and his role in the creation of the world has parallels with myths in several early cultures. The emergence of the frost giant from the void and the way he produced offspring both mirror ancient Greek accounts of the primordial earth goddess Gaia. The Greek creation story also involved a gaping void, known

Left: This 19th-century book illustration depicts a meeting between the frost giant Ymir and the small but powerful figure of the god Thor.

created the earth by ripping apart the monstrous goddess Tlaltecuhtli. The two gods used the goddess's head and shoulders to form the earth, and the remainder of her corpse to form the sky. In the Rig Veda, meanwhile, Manu, the first man, sacrificed the giant Purusa and created the world from his remains.

Sources and inspirations

Like so many other Norse myths, the most extensive account of Ymir's existence and death is in Snorri Sturluson's *Prose Edda*, which was probably written around 1220. Snorri presented the story of Ymir in the context of a meeting between Gylfi, a king of Sweden, and three mysterious wise men, all of whom have Odin-like characteristics. Gylfi asks the three figures many questions about the history of the world, to which they provide answers before disappearing. Snorri, it is clear, drew on a number of earlier sources when writing the wise men's answers to Gylfi's questions about Ymir. The poem *Völuspá*, which is part of the *Poetic Edda* and dates from around 1000, gave Snorri the concept of Ginnungagap and the outline of the story of the three gods who raised up the earth and created Midgard. Two other poems, which scholars believe may have been composed in Norway in the 9th or 10th centuries, describe how Ymir came into being, the children he created, and his fate at the hands of Odin, Vili, and Vé. One of them, "Vafthrúdnismál," contains an account of how the giant's bones, blood, and skull become the mountains, seas, and sky, while the other, "Grímnismál," details how Ymir's hair became the trees and his brains the clouds.

While parts of the Ymir myth may be derived from ancient Indo-European legends, one aspect of the story roots it firmly in the environment and cultures of Scandinavia. The emergence of the giant from the meeting of steam and ice reflects the paramount significance of heat and cold to the Norse peoples.

ANDREW CAMPBELL

as Chaos, that existed before anything else. Gaia came into existence soon after Chaos, and from an act of parthenogenesis gave birth to Uranus (the sky), Pontus (the oceans), and Ourea (the mountains). The notion of a younger generation of divine beings overthrowing an older generation is also found in Greek mythology, with the victory of the Olympians, led by Zeus, over the Titans.

Creation myths in which a divine being's corpse forms the physical world also feature in other ancient cultures. The Babylonian epic *Enuma Elish* (c. 1900 BCE) describes the battle between the god Marduk and the goddess dragon Tiamat. After slaughtering Tiamat, Marduk slices her body in two—he thrusts one half upward to form the sky and the other half down to form the earth. The Aztecs of Mexico told of a myth in which two of their most important gods—the multifaceted feathered serpent god Quetzalcoatl and the warrior god Tezcatlipoca—

Bibliography

Davidson, H. R. Ellis. *Scandinavian Mythology*. London: Hamlyn, 1982.
Snorri Sturluson, and Anthony Faulkes, trans. *Edda*. New York: Oxford University Press, 1991.

SEE ALSO: Bor; Búri; Creation Myths; Odin; Quetzalcoatl; Scandinavia; Tiamat.

ZEUS

In Greek mythology, Zeus was supreme god of the cosmos, which he ruled from Mount Olympus. Ancient Greeks believed he was god of justice, because he could look down from the heavens and see everything that people did. His special bird was the eagle, king of birds. As god of the sky, Zeus sent rains down on the earth. His favorite weapon was the thunderbolt.

Below: Zeus sits on his throne amid the other Olympian gods in a frieze on a civic building in Athens, Greece.

Zeus did not start out as supreme ruler of the universe—he had to win that position from his father, Cronus, and wrest his power from Titans and earthborn Giants. Once he had gained the divine throne, however, Zeus became the unchallenged leader of the Olympians, the major divinities of the Greek world for more than 600 years.

According to tradition, Cronus, a Titan, overcame his father Uranus and was determined to remain in power. When Cronus learned that he was destined to be overthrown by his son, he took drastic steps to prevent the prophecy from coming true. Every time his, wife, Rhea gave birth to a child, Cronus swallowed the infant. When he had devoured two sons, Poseidon and Hades—and in some versions of the legend also three daughters, Hestia, Demeter, and Hera—Rhea turned to her mother, Gaia, for help in thwarting her husband. Together they came up with a plan.

The Age of Zeus

Zeus is an ancient deity, but historians were not sure quite how early he was worshiped until archaeological excavations beneath the foundations of a house at Palaikastro in the northeast corner of Crete uncovered the altar of a temple dedicated to the Greek god. Within the earthworks they found evidence of cult practices that had continued from the eighth century BCE until the Roman conquest of the island in 67 BCE. In the surrounding area they uncovered an inscription, broken in many pieces, that contained a hymn to Zeus, and several antefixae (carved ornaments on a roof) in the shape of lion heads. The Cretan sanctuary is thought to have been plundered by Christians at the end of the fourth century CE.

When Rhea gave birth to her third son, Zeus, she gave Cronus a stone wrapped in a baby blanket, which he at once swallowed. Rhea meanwhile hid the real baby in a cave on Mount Dicte (or Mount Ida) on the island of Crete. There the goat Amaltheia gave him milk, and the Curetes—a brotherhood of Cretans—banged their bronze shields to conceal the baby's crying. Thus did Zeus escape his father and grow to manhood in secrecy.

When Zeus came of age, he conspired with Rhea or Gaia to give Cronus a drug that forced him to disgorge all the children he had swallowed. The divine offspring emerged fully grown from their father's stomach, and they all immediately joined Zeus in a battle against Cronus and the other Titans. Only two Titans sided with Zeus: Prometheus and Oceanus. The Cyclopes (one-eyed giants) and the Hecatoncheires (three giant sons of Uranus and Gaia who each had 100 arms and 50 heads) were dug up from the earth, in which Uranus had buried them, and they also fought alongside Zeus. In a war that lasted 10 years, the Titans were defeated and sent down below the earth to Tartarus. Zeus then divided the world among his brothers. Claiming the sky for himself, he allotted the sea to Poseidon and the underworld to Hades.

Before the new deities could assume power, however, they had to fight one more battle. Gaia, angry that the Giants had been given no portion of the world, roused them to battle against Zeus. After another 10-year struggle, Zeus and his brothers defeated the Giants, as well as Typhon, a monster created by Gaia. Depending on different

Left: Olive groves on the slopes of Mount Ida in Crete. It was here that Zeus was brought up in secret.

versions of the myth, either Typhon was imprisoned by Zeus under Mount Etna, a volcano in Sicily, or thrown into Tartarus. Once the Titans, the forces of barbarism, and the Giants, the agents of unrestrained violence, had been defeated, a new pantheon could take over the universe. They settled on Mount Olympus, and hence became known as the Olympians.

Versatile god

In the Greek pantheon Zeus was originally a sky god, a weather deity who sent rain and who, when angry, hurled lightning and thunderbolts. On Mount Olympus he gathered the clouds about his throne and watched the actions of mortals on earth. In time, his role developed and he became the guiding deity for various aspects of civilized life in ancient Greece. When Greeks took oaths, they swore to Zeus; and it was Zeus who made sure that both parties kept their word. Thus Zeus upheld law and justice among men. He was invoked as the god of marriage, Zeus Teleios; and in times of need, he was a savior, Zeus Soter. He was also god of guests, Zeus Xenios (see box, page 1434).

Above: This painting by French artist Nicolas Poussin (1594–1665) shows the infant Zeus being fed with milk from the goat Amaltheia.

In art, Zeus is almost always pictured as a strong and fit male, usually with a beard. He often holds in his hand a thunderbolt and carries a shield made of goatskin. This was known as his aegis: in modern English, "to be under someone's aegis" means to be under his or her protection. In time Zeus lent his aegis to his favorite daughter, Athena, and it became a regular part of her attire. In images of Zeus seated on his throne, his bird, the eagle, appears perched on the god's scepter. Oak trees, towering into the sky, were sacred to Zeus. At Dodona in northwestern Greece, the rustling of oak leaves was said to tell the word of Zeus. Priests resided there to interpret these rustlings.

Amorous god

Zeus was an amorous god, and there are numerous legends about his affairs with gods and humans. Although they make great stories—they involve many disguises and subterfuges to escape detection—the tales also have symbolic significance. Since in the polytheistic belief system

Below: Based on an ancient Greek original, this marble statue of Zeus was sculpted in the first century CE.

Hospitality

One of the most important human activities over which Zeus presided was hospitality. As Zeus Xenios, God of Guest-Friendship, he made sure that the trust necessary between host and guest was fully honored. In a world without regular hotels or inns, travelers expected to be taken in wherever they found themselves at the end of the day, whether it was a humble hut or a regal palace. Since it may be dangerous to let a stranger into one's house, the Greeks made sure that this temporary but important relationship was protected by their chief god. Many great legends of Greek mythology turn on violations of hospitality and the vengeance brought on those who abuse the kindness of the host or the trust of the visitor.

of ancient Greece there was no single deity who brought things to life, many of the beings, forces, and materials essential to human existence were believed to have been the product of unions between two deities or between a deity and a mortal. Zeus would mate in order to engender what the world needed. In early days, since there were few male and female figures in Greek mythology, these alliances were often made between brother and sister or others who were closely related. This behavior was not tolerated by Greeks among mortals but was considered acceptable for the early gods.

The birth of Athena

According to some stories, when Zeus found out that his first love, the Titan Metis (Thought), was destined to bear a child mightier than its father, he swallowed the pregnant mother. Zeus then developed a headache that could be relieved only when his skull was split with an ax. While versions vary as to who wielded the ax, nearly every account agrees that, once the blow was landed, it was Athena, fully developed and armed, who sprang from the head of Zeus. Others reject the Metis story and have Athena herself claiming that she had no mother. In these versions, she sprang from Zeus's head as a tangible representation of her father's divine thought. Athena was her father's favorite child. She shared with him not only his aegis but also the secret of where he kept the thunderbolts and

Right: This marble frieze showing the marriage of Zeus and Hera stands on the wall of a temple at Selinunte, an ancient Greek city in Sicily.

how to use them. As goddess of wisdom and creative crafts, it is appropriate that Athena should have appeared from the head of the king of gods and men.

Zeus also made alliances with other Titan females. Themis, daughter of Uranus and Gaia, bore him the Horae, three goddesses who made the seasons change. Their names were Eunomia (Good Order), Dike (Justice), and Eirene (Peace). She also gave birth to the three Fates, Clotho, Lachesis, and Atropos. From Zeus's alliance with Mnemosyne, goddess of memory, were born the nine Muses—Calliope, Clio, Erato, Euterpe, Melpomene, Polyhymnia, Terpsichore, Thalia, and Urania. The offspring of Zeus's affair with Leto, daughter of Coeus and Phoebe, were sun god Apollo and goddess of hunting Artemis.

Zeus mated with lesser divinities as well. From his liaison with the sea nymph Eurynome were born the three Graces, whom Greek poet Hesiod (fl. 800 BCE) named Aglaiea (Splendor), Euphrosyne (Joy), and Thalia (Bloom). On another occasion the nymph Maia caught Zeus's roving eye; from their union Hermes was born. Zeus was on the point of having an affair with Thetis, but just in time Prometheus warned him that any child the sea nymph bore would be more powerful than his father. To prevent being part of this outcome, Zeus married Thetis off to the mortal Peleus; she later gave birth to Achilles.

Formidable wife

Zeus's wife or consort was his sister, Hera. Through her marriage to Zeus she became an important goddess who looked after the lives of married women. With Zeus she produced at least three children: Hebe, goddess of youth; Eileithyia, goddess of childbirth; and Ares, god of war. While some say there was a fourth child of the union, Hephaestus, god of fire, the more common version is that Hera produced him on her own as a reprisal against Zeus for his solo creation of Athena. However, unlike Athena, Hephaestus was born lame: his legs were deformed, and his body misshapen. Disgusted by her son's appearance, and angry at her own ineptitude, Hera threw Hephaestus off Mount Olympus, and he landed on the island of Lemnos. According to other accounts, however, it was not Hera who expelled Hephaestus but Zeus himself. Either way, fire was needed in the Greek world, and so was its patron deity. Hephaestus was restored to Mount Olympus, and there he married Aphrodite, goddess of love.

In addition to goddesses and nymphs, Zeus was attracted to many mortals. One of the first human females he pursued was Europa, daughter of Agenor, king of Tyre. In order to get close to her, Zeus turned himself into a beautiful white bull and pranced into the meadow where Europa and her sisters were tending the family herd. Fascinated by the fine animal, Europa climbed on its back. At once the bull dashed into the sea and carried the princess off to Crete. There he revealed his true identity and intentions. In time Europa gave birth to Minos— according to tradition, the Minoan culture on Crete is named for him. Two other children were also born from this couple: Rhadamanthys, who after his reign of Phaistos on Crete became a judge in the underworld, and the third son, Sarpedon. Stories of Sarpedon vary: in one of the best known he went off to Asia Minor (modern Turkey) to rule over the people of Lycia.

Io, a priestess of Hera, was another mortal who attracted Zeus. She was lured by the god into a grove outside the city of Argos. In some versions of the myth, when Hera caught sight of the two lovers, she immediately turned Io into a white cow. In others it was Zeus who changed Io into a cow that Hera then asked to have for her own. In either case, Io remained a cow and Hera sent Argus, a 100-

eyed giant, to watch over her. Hermes, assigned by Zeus to rescue Io, lulled all of Argus's eyes to sleep with music and then cut off his head. Argus became a peacock or, in another version, his eyes were transplanted by Hera onto the peacock's tail. When Io was rescued, Hera sent a stinging gadfly to torment her. The cow girl fled across the Bosporus, the strait between Europe and Asia in modern Turkey, a place whose name means "cow crossing." Io went on to Egypt, where Zeus finally restored her to human form. From his touch she gave birth to a son, Epaphus, who would become the founder of the Egyptian race.

Alcmene of Thebes was also ravished by Zeus, even though she had just married Amphitryon, son of Alcaeus, king of Tiryns, a town in the eastern Peloponnese. Alcmene told her new husband that she would not go to his bed until he had avenged wrongs done to her brothers. While Amphitryon was off on this mission, Zeus came to Alcmene's bed in the form of Amphitryon himself.

Alcmene, thinking her husband was safely home, agreed at last to sleep with him. She was shocked when later that night her true mortal husband returned. As a result of the double union, Alcmene gave birth to two children: Iphicles, son of Amphitryon, and Heracles, son of Zeus. Hera did everything in her power to destroy this child of her husband's, but every time Heracles escaped her plots.

Zeus and Danae, Leda, and Semele

There was nothing a mortal could do to resist the attentions of Zeus. Acrisius, king of Argos, had been warned by the Delphic oracle that his daughter Danae would give birth to a son who would one day kill his grandfather. In an effort to prevent the omen from coming to pass, Acrisius immediately imprisoned his daughter in an underground chamber made of bronze with only a small aperture for light and air. No man could come in, and she could not go out. As Danae mourned the loss of her freedom, she noticed a strange, sunny glow creeping through the window. Gradually the glow coalesced into a shower of gold, and then into the form of Zeus. He was attracted to the imprisoned girl and determined to be her lover. Danae naturally felt little loyalty to her father at this point and saw no reason why she should not have an affair with this handsome divinity. Later she gave birth to a son, Perseus. Acrisius shut mother and child into a chest and threw it into the sea. The chest was washed ashore, and Perseus grew to manhood on the island of Seriphos. When he returned to Argos to take part in athletic contests there, his throw of the discus went wide and struck Acrisius among the watching bystanders. Thus did Perseus kill his grandfather, and thus was destiny fulfilled. Some stories say that Perseus lived on to establish the citadel at Mycenae.

The most unusual story of Zeus and a mortal woman is that of his relationship with Leda, queen of Sparta. This time the god embarked on his seduction in the form of a large white swan. As a result of her union with the swan, Leda laid either one or two eggs. From these hatched two daughters, Helen and Clytemnestra, and two sons, Castor and Pollux. Helen and Pollux were children of Zeus; Clytemnestra and Castor were fathered by Leda's mortal husband, Tyndareos.

Semele, daughter of Cadmus, king of Thebes, also attracted Zeus's interest. The god appeared to her as a mortal lover. Hera, aware of her husband's infidelity, disguised herself as Semele's maid and persuaded the princess to ask her lover to reveal his true power. Having promised Semele that he would answer any request, Zeus was compelled to show his true form. While demonstrating his lightning, he unleashed a bolt which consumed Semele in its flames. Zeus snatched the unborn child from her ashes and sewed it into his own thigh. In time the baby was born from the thigh of Zeus. Dionysus was thus a god of double birth whose mortality had been burned away in Zeus's fire. In all of Greek mythology, Dionysus was the only child of a union between mortal and god who was immortal and fully divine.

Divine power

Not all stories of Zeus concern the god's amatory adventures. Many tell of his unrivaled power. In the conflict for supremacy between Zeus and the Titans, Prometheus supported Zeus and for a time was his chief counselor. Later, over the question of how to apportion a sacrificial animal justly between the gods and humans, he devised

ATHENS 2004

a plan by which humans received the choicest parts. Angered, Zeus denied humanity the gift of fire proposed by Prometheus, fearing that its use for making tools and weapons would cause mortals to consider themselves the equals of the gods. Prometheus, however, stole fire from the hearth of Zeus and carried it to Earth in a fennel stalk. (In another version of the legend, Prometheus took fire from the forge of Hephaestus.)

As punishment Zeus ordered Prometheus to be chained to a rock on Mount Caucasus, where he underwent the daily torment of an eagle devouring his liver, which grew back each night. Throughout his ordeal Prometheus taunted Zeus with a secret, known only to him: that the goddess Thetis, who was being courted by Zeus, would give birth to a son who would grow up to be mightier than his father. In fact, this mortal was the Greek hero Achilles, who grew up to be a greater warrior than his mortal father Peleus.

In another legend, Zeus ordered the creation of a woman to plague Prometheus and all men. Pandora was endowed with alluring graces and furnished with a magic jar (Pandora's box). Suspecting trickery, Prometheus refused to accept her, but his brother Epimetheus gladly took her

Above: The remains of the great temple of Olympian Zeus still stand in Athens. The building originally had 104 columns.

as his wife. Succumbing to temptation, Pandora opened the jar, whereupon all the evils and diseases that came to afflict mortals were released. By the time the jar was closed, only Hope remained inside, so humans had ills but no hope.

In another story, Zeus grew angry when Asclepius, son of Apollo and god of healing, brought a mortal back to life. He hurled Asclepius down to the realm of the dead. Although Asclepius was later returned to the earth so that he could continue curing humans, he never ascended Mount Olympus because he was too busy serving mortals as divine physician.

Zeus ruled from Mount Olympus but had sanctuaries in many parts of Greece. The most famous of these was at Olympia in the western Peloponnese, where the Olympic Games were held in his honor every four years. Athletes competed in honor of Zeus for a crown of olive leaves. The men offered their best gift, their physical ability, to the god whose rule was supreme. Greeks used the span between Olympic festivals as their dating system: events in Greek history were measured in Olympiads, four-year periods from 776 BCE. The stadia where the contests were held became the standard unit of measurement: distances between cities were measured not in miles but in stadia,

units of approximately 600 feet (185 m). For the temple to Zeus at Olympia, Greek sculptor Phidias (fl. c. 490–430 BCE) carved a statue from gold and ivory measuring 42 feet (12.8 m) in height. It was one of the Seven Wonders of the Ancient World. Athletic contests were also held in Zeus's honor at Nemea, near Corinth, every two years. At Nemea the athletic events were similar to those at Olympia, only here the winner won a crown made of the soft dark green leaves of watercress.

KARELISA HARTIGAN

Bibliography

Aeschylus, and Robert Fagles, trans. *The Oresteia*. New York: Penguin USA, 1984.

Bulfinch, Thomas. *Bulfinch's Mythology*. New York: Modern Library, 1998.

Hesiod, and M. L. West, trans. *Theogony; and Works and Days*. New York: Oxford University Press, 1999.

Homer, and Robert Fagles, trans. *The Iliad*. New York: Penguin USA, 2003.

Howatson, M. C., and Ian Chilvers. *Concise Oxford Companion to Classical Literature*. New York: Oxford University Press, 1993.

SEE ALSO: Aphrodite; Ares; Asclepius; Athena; Castor and Pollux; Clytemnestra; Cronus; Cyclopes; Danae; Demeter; Dionysus; Europa; Fates; Gaia; Giants; Graces; Greece; Hades; Hebe; Helen; Hephaestus; Hera; Heracles; Hermes; Hestia; Leda; Minos; Mnemosyne; Muses; Pandora; Perseus; Poseidon; Prometheus; Thetis; Titans; Typhon; Uranus.

INDEX

Page numbers in *italics* refer to
picture captions. Page numbers
in **bold** refer to main articles.